FAR EAST

A R Gurney

BROADWAY PLAY PUBLISHING INC
56 E 81st St., NY NY 10028-0202
212 772-8334 fax: 212 772-8358
http://www.BroadwayPlayPubl.com

First printing: June 1999
ISBN: 0-88145-161-4

Book design: Marie Donovan
Typographic controls: Xerox Ventura Publisher 2.0 P E
Typeface: Palatino
Copy editing: Liam Brosnahan
Printed on recycled acid-free paper and bound in the U S A.

ABOUT THE AUTHOR

A R Gurney has been writing plays for most of his life.
Among his many works are THE DINING ROOM,
THE COCKTAIL HOUR, LOVE LETTERS, and
SYLVIA. He lives in Connecticut and New York City.

To Daniel Sullivan
With many thanks for getting it all together

FAR EAST was first produced at the Williamstown
Theater Festival, Michael Ritchie, Producer, opening on
15 July 1998. The cast and creative contributors were:

READER ....Tohoru Masamune
"SPARKY" WATTS,
Lieutenant (j.g.), U S N R ....Scott Wolf
JAMES ANDERSON, Captain, U S N .....Bill Smitrovich
JULIA ....Linda Emond
BOB MUNGER, Ensign, U S N R .... Paul Fitzgerald
PERCUSSIONIST .... Pun Boonyarata-Pun
STAGEHANDS ....David Mason, José Sanchez,
                       Lisa Schmon, & Olevia White

Director .... Daniel Sullivan
Sets .... Michael Brown
Costumes .... Danielle Castronovo
Lighting ....Rui Rita
Production stage manager .... Grayson Meritt

FAR EAST open on 11 January 1999 in the Mitzi E Newhouse Theater at Lincoln Center; André Bishop, Artistic Director; Bernard Gersten, Executive Producer. The cast and creative contributors were:

STAGEHANDS Mia Tagano & Toshiro Akira Yamamoto
READER . . . . Sonnie Brown
"SPARKY" WATTS,
Lieutenant (j.g.), U S N R . . . . Michael Hayden
JAMES ANDERSON, Captain, U S N . . . . . Bill Smitrovich
JULIA . . . . Lisa Emery
BOB MUNGER, Ensign, U S N R . . . . . Connor Trinneer
PERCUSSIONIST-MUSICIAN . . . . Carlos Valdez

Director . . . . Daniel Sullivan
Sets . . . . Thomas Lynch
Costumes . . . . Jess Goldstein
Lighting . . . . Rui Rita
Original music and sound . . . . Dan Moses Schreier
Stage manager . . . . Roy Harris
Casting . . . . Daniel Swee
Director of marketing . . . . Thomas Cott
Director of development . . . . Hattie K Jutagir
General manager . . . . Steven C Callahan
Production manager . . . . Jeff Hamlin
Assistant stage manager . . . . Janet Takami

CHARACTERS AND SETTING

JAMES ANDERSON, *Captain, U S N*
JULIA, *his wife*
"SPARKY" WATTS, *Lieutenant (j.g.), U S N R*
BOB MUNGER, *Ensign, U S N R*
READER, *female*
DRUMMER, *male or female*
Two STAGEHANDS, *male or female*

Japan: July 1954–October 1955

NOTES ON SET AND STAGING

The playing area should project, if possible, into the audience as it does in Kabuki or Noh drama. Similarly, the scenery should invoke the simplicity and style of Japanese theater. Traveling screens or drops may be used to define various settings as well as to mask entrances and exits.

Above, or off to one side, is a low wooden lectern with a simple wooden stool behind it. This is similar to the station of the Chanter in Bunraku puppet drama or of the narrator in Kabuki. Here, the role should be played by an Asian woman, to be called the READER, since she reads all her parts from a script on the lectern. (This lectern should be placed or constructed so that the audience can't count pages. Ideally, the READER would kneel on pillows before it, but it is doubtful that many actors could last in this position for the length of the play.) The other actors do not look at the READER during exchanges of dialogue, but rather play as if the voice is coming from elsewhere.

The READER also uses two wooden blocks, which she clacks together to indicate shifts in place or time, as may happen in Kabuki drama. Near her is a small radio, suggesting the 1950s, which she turns on when indicated. Behind the READER is a PERCUSSIONIST to add sound effects on a Japanese *taiko* drum or other Asian instruments. The PERCUSSIONIST may be visible, though it might be less distracting if he or she were hidden behind a screen. Additional Japanese and American music and sound are also used.

The READER wears a kimono and white *tabi* on her feet. The PERCUSSIONIST wears black, loose-fitting Japanese *hapi* coat and slacks, with black *tabi*. These dark clothes are also worn by two STAGEHANDS, who silently add or remove props and furniture as needed, and who may also help move screens. They may also wear thin black veils, obscuring their faces. The American characters, of course, wear uniforms or costumes appropriate for the fifties.

All furniture should look simple and abstracted, and have multiple uses. Stools serve as chairs or tables, couches become beds, and so forth.

The overall purpose of these various devices is not to be arty or exotic, but rather to suggest the fluid, unfamiliar, and subservient world within which the play occurs.

ACT ONE

(At lights to half:)

(Exotic Japanese music from a woodwind instrument)

(The DRUMMER *and* STAGEHANDS *enter and take their positions. Then the* READER *enters, carrying the script of the play in an elegant cover. She sits or kneels and places the script carefully on the lectern, opens it, then clacks her blocks together.* DRUMMER *produces a series of rapid beats.* "SPARKY" WATTS *appears, in dress khakis of a Naval officer. His shoulder bars indicate that he is a Lieutenant Junior Grade. He carries his orders in an official-looking manila envelope. The* READER *turns on her radio. The Japanese music modulates to the sound of Jo Stafford singing:)*

"See the pyramids along the Nile,
Watch the sunrise on a tropic isle,
But, just remember, darling, all the while,
You Belong to Me..."

(A STAGEHAND *places a stool.* SPARKY *sits. The song gives way to the sound of an airplane engine.* SPARKY *holds his hat, looks out the window of the "plane" as the screens open to reveal a Japanese landscape painting.)*

(The READER *clacks again. The sound fades away.)*

READER: *(Reading in a Japanese accent)* The American Naval base at Yokosuka, Japan, fifty miles south of Tokyo. Office of Strategic Planning. July. Nineteen Fifty-Four.

*(*SPARKY *leaves the "plane".)*

SPARKY: *(As if to a sailor on duty)* Watts reporting for duty.

READER: *(In an American accent)* The Captain wants to see you, Mr Watts.

SPARKY: The Captain? When?

READER: Whenever you showed up, sir.

SPARKY: Then here I am.

(Clack)

(A STAGEHAND *takes the envelope, hands it to* CAPTAIN JAMES ANDERSON *as he enters. He also wears dress khakis. His insignia indicate he is a captain in the U S Navy, the wings on his breast pocket show that he is also a flyer, and his ribbons suggest that he has been in a number of battles. Simultaneously,* STAGEHANDS *set up a table and chair to form his desk, as a map of Japan and Korea drops in behind.)*

READER: Lieutenant Watts is here, sir.

ANDERSON: Send him in.

READER: You may go in, sir.

(Clack)

*(*SPARKY *enters the "office".)*

ANDERSON: *(Sitting at desk, reading from orders)* Lieutenant Junior Grade Wallace W Watts.

SPARKY: That's me.

ANDERSON: *(Looks up)* What do you call that?

SPARKY: What do I call what, sir?

ANDERSON: Wallace W Watts. Three double-u's. What did they call that at... *(Glances at file)* ...Princeton.

SPARKY: Oh. Alliteration, sir.

ANDERSON: Alliteration.

SPARKY: But most people call me Sparky.

ANDERSON: They don't.

SPARKY: They do. Sparky Watts. Get it?

ANDERSON: I do.

SPARKY: It's better than Wallace. Or Wally.
Wally Watts? Thanks but no thanks.

ANDERSON: I see what you mean.

SPARKY: My mother thought up Sparky, actually.
She thinks I'm a live wire.

ANDERSON: I'll call you Mr Watts, Mr Watts.

SPARKY: Yes, sir.

ANDERSON: Welcome to the Far East.

SPARKY: Thank you, sir.

ANDERSON: Where have you been?

SPARKY: Been?

ANDERSON: (Checking his orders) You were supposed to
report over a week ago.

SPARKY: Oh. I put in for additional leave, sir.
Permission attached.

ANDERSON: Why the additional leave? You already
took a sizeable chunk of travel time.

SPARKY: I wanted to get my bearings, sir.

ANDERSON: Get. Your. Bearings... Good nautical
expression.

SPARKY: Thank you, sir.

ANDERSON: Did you get them?

SPARKY: Well, first I checked out Tokyo. And then
I hopped a train up to the famous mountain resort
of Hakone, where they're filming James Michener's
The Bridges at Toko-Ri, starring William Holden and
Grace Kelly. I met William Holden, actually. I shook
hands with him.

ANDERSON: Did William Holden give you your bearings?

SPARKY: *(Reaching into his pocket)* No. But he gave me a souvenir Zippo lighter. Want to see it?

ANDERSON: No, thanks. *(Looking at orders again)* I notice you checked into the Bachelor Officers' Quarters after working hours on Friday.

SPARKY: I figured I'd take the weekend to settle in.

ANDERSON: And did you?

SPARKY: Yes sir. Everything's copacetic.

ANDERSON: Where were you last night?

SPARKY: Last night?

ANDERSON: The Fourth of July picnic at the Officer's Club.

SPARKY: Uh-oh.

ANDERSON: Attendance mandatory.

SPARKY: It slipped my mind, sir.

ANDERSON: The Fourth of July slipped your mind?

SPARKY: The picnic, sir.

ANDERSON: We take our national holidays seriously in the Far East, Mr Watts. Stationed halfway around the globe, the truce in Korea hanging by a thread, we like to remind ourselves why we're here.

SPARKY: Yes, sir.

ANDERSON: We posted a special notice on the B O Q bulletin board.

SPARKY: I wasn't in the B O Q last night, sir.

ANDERSON: I thought you were settled in.

SPARKY: I had a date last night, sir.

ANDERSON: A date.

SPARKY: Off the base.

ANDERSON: So, instead of celebrating our nation's independence, you decided to celebrate your own.

SPARKY: Good way of putting it, sir.

ANDERSON: You haven't wasted much time. Hardly a week in Japan and you've found yourself a girl.

SPARKY: I lucked out, sir.

(A STAGEHAND *brings* ANDERSON *coffee on a Japanese lacquered tray.)*

ANDERSON: *(To* SPARKY*)* Want coffee?

SPARKY: Sure.

ANDERSON: *(To* STAGEHAND*)* Get him coffee.

READER: Aye, aye, sir.

ANDERSON: *(To* SPARKY*)* Want anything in it?

SPARKY: Everything.

ANDERSON: *(To* STAGEHAND*)* The man wants everything.

READER: Aye, aye, sir.

*(*STAGEHAND *goes, with tray.)*

ANDERSON: My wife missed you last night, Mr Watts.

SPARKY: Your wife?

ANDERSON: She thinks she knows you. Or knows your family. She saw your name on the list of new officers. You're from Minneapolis?

SPARKY: Milwaukee, sir.

ANDERSON: She found some connection.

SPARKY: I didn't know that, sir.

ANDERSON: So she was disappointed. Since she arranged the whole affair. Stateside beer, hot dogs, the whole nine yards. She even rounded up some American girls.

SPARKY: Sounds great, sir.

ANDERSON: She thinks junior officers stationed in the Orient can become...disoriented.

SPARKY: That's a good one.

ANDERSON: Yes, well, she likes to remind them of home.

SPARKY: I hope you'll convey my apologies to your wife, sir.

(A STAGEHAND *brings* SPARKY *a mug of coffee.*)

ANDERSON: Here's your coffee.

SPARKY: *(Taking it)* Thanks.

ANDERSON: How long have you been in the Navy, Mr Watts?

SPARKY: Two years, if you count Officers' Candidate School at Newport, sir.

ANDERSON: Why should I count that? Four quick months, and they hand you a commission.

SPARKY: Four *tough* months, sir.

ANDERSON: The Naval Academy takes four tough *years.*

SPARKY: I know that, sir.

ANDERSON: Plus a six-week training cruise every summer.

SPARKY: Yes, sir.

ANDERSON: Plus an additional eighteen months of flight school if you want to fly.

SPARKY: I have great respect for Academy men, sir.

ANDERSON: Why thank you, Mr Watts.

(A STAGEHAND *brings* ANDERSON *documents on a clipboard, which he reads and signs as he talks.*)

ANDERSON: Why did you join the Navy?

SPARKY: There was a war going on.

ANDERSON: What? Oh, you mean that little skirmish in Korea? Which Truman called a police action? Where we lost over fifty thousand boys and ended right where we started? That little episode?

SPARKY: It's America's job to protect the Free World, sir.

ANDERSON: That why you joined?

SPARKY: That's certainly part of it.

ANDERSON: What's the other part?

SPARKY: I would have been drafted.

ANDERSON: If you had been, you'd be home by now.

SPARKY: I wanted to be an officer, sir. So I'd get more experience.

ANDERSON: Experience.

SPARKY: Frankly, sir, I come from a pretty sheltered background. I feel I could benefit from some significant life experiences in the world at large.

ANDERSON: Had any?

SPARKY: Sir, I have lucked out from the word go. You'll see from my file that after Newport I had a tour of duty as Assistant Gunnery Officer aboard the cruiser *Worcester* in the Mediterranean, patrolling the soft underbelly of Western Europe.

ANDERSON: Go on.

SPARKY: I was in charge of a deck division of thirty men. Our gun turret won two citations for target practice.

ANDERSON: Congratulations.

SPARKY: And my collateral duties were in Special Services. I organized several overnight tours for enlisted men, to enjoy the cultural advantages of Paris and Rome.

ANDERSON: Ah.

SPARKY: And when we came into Salonika, Greece, I led seventy-three sailors on a special climb up Mount Olympus. *(Shows him a picture from his wallet)*

ANDERSON: Did you lead them down again?

SPARKY: I did. With the help of some local donkeys I commandeered for the occasion.

ANDERSON: And now you've saved western Europe, you want to protect Japan.

SPARKY: I wanted a change, sir, so I applied for shore duty in the Far East. And got it! I left my ship at Naples and hopped on whatever military air transportation was heading this way. And I stopped wherever I could, to see as much as possible of the postwar world and America's place in it.

ANDERSON: Have any significant life experiences along the way?

SPARKY: A few.

ANDERSON: Have one last night?

SPARKY: I don't have to answer that, sir.

ANDERSON: You're right.

(A STAGEHAND brings ANDERSON his jacket, hat, and briefcase)

READER: Staff meeting in five minutes, Captain.

ANDERSON: Roger. When do you get out, Mr Watts?

SPARKY: On or about December 6th of next year. Unless I get released early in time to further my education at Graduate School.

ANDERSON: *(Putting on his jacket)* Courtesy of the G I Bill of Rights.

SPARKY: With that, and what I saved at sea, I'll never have to ask my folks for another dime.

ANDERSON: Any Graduate School in mind?

SPARKY: The Harvard Business School.

ANDERSON: Ah.

SPARKY: If I can get in. They say being a Naval officer is a major plus on your resume.

ANDERSON: We help when we can.... Did you take Naval Etiquette during your four tough months at Newport?

SPARKY: I did, sir.

ANDERSON: Did they teach you to leave a calling card at the residence of your commanding officer?

SPARKY: I don't have a calling card, sir.

ANDERSON: You can get one printed up, on the beach.

SPARKY: Yes, sir.

ANDERSON: Write a note on the back. Apologizing to my wife. (*Hands* SPARKY's *orders to* STAGEHAND; *gets his hat*)

SPARKY: Oh, O K.

ANDERSON: And fold down the upper right-hand corner.

SPARKY: May I ask why, sir?

ANDERSON: It means that no response is required.

SPARKY: Gotcha, sir.

(ANDERSON *starts out again, again stops.*)

ANDERSON: Remind me what your orders are.

SPARKY: To help plan the evacuation of non-Communist troops and civilians from the northern part of French Indochina. I see it as an important project, sir. Now that the French have lost the battle of Dien Bien Phu.

ANDERSON: You see it as a significant life experience?

SPARKY: I do, sir.

ANDERSON: Then go experience it.

SPARKY: Aye aye, sir.

(SPARKY *and* ANDERSON *go off either way.*)

(*Clack*)

(*Japanese music:* STAGEHANDS *bring on a low day bed and remove the desk.* JULIA *comes on, carrying a Japanese flower arrangement. She is younger than* ANDERSON. *She puts the arrangement on a stool.*)

JULIA: What do you think, Noriko?

READER: Very pretty, Okusama.

JULIA: Did I get the symbolism right? All three elements in balance? Earth, sky, man?

READER: Oh, yes.

JULIA: (*Fingering a dangling fern*) Why does "man" always look slightly pathetic? (*She tries to adjust it.*) I don't know, Noriko. Maybe I'm better at throwing great bunches of American wild flowers into some Paul Revere bowl.

(ANDERSON'*s voice off:* "Hello!")

READER: Captain-san here.

(ANDERSON *comes in, with briefcase.*)

ANDERSON: Hi, babe.

JULIA: Home is the sailor.

(*They kiss.*)

ANDERSON: Home is the pencil-pusher.

JULIA: That'll be all, Noriko. Thank you. (*Indicating flowers*) She's teaching me the ancient art of flower arranging.

ANDERSON: Looks good.

JULIA: It's supposed to mean something terribly significant. But I can't seem to connect the dots. Maybe I should try something else. Like the Japanese tea ceremony. Or the subtleties of combat karate.

(A STAGEHAND *brings a drink on a tray.)*

*(*JULIA *hands the drink to* ANDERSON, *after putting his hat on the tray.)*

ANDERSON: Suit yourself.

JULIA: *(Producing a calling card)* Speaking of ceremonies, is this your doing?

ANDERSON: Damn right.

JULIA: It arrived in the middle of our Book Club meeting. We were discussing "The Naked and the Dead", when lo and behold! A calling card!

ANDERSON: Did the kid chew your ear off?

JULIA: He wasn't there.

ANDERSON: Wasn't *there?*

JULIA: Some sailor delivered it.

ANDERSON: He sends a sailor with his personal calling card?

JULIA: Apparently he had a tennis game.

ANDERSON: Oh, Christ!

JULIA: It's all right, Jim.

ANDERSON: It's all wrong, for Chrissake.

JULIA: I suppose you expected him to place it on a silver tray in the front hall.

ANDERSON: That's the tradition, as a matter of fact. He should have presented himself.

JULIA: This isn't Annapolis, Jim. And we're not still fighting the War of 1812.

ANDERSON: The nerve of the guy!

JULIA: I'll bet you would have done the same thing yourself. In your fly-boy days.

ANDERSON: Send a sailor? Hell no! I would have sent a Marine.

JULIA: He wrote a very sweet note on the back. *(Reading)* "I apologize for my absence on the 4th. I have no excuse but my own negligence."

ANDERSON: He didn't neglect some B-girl on the beach.

JULIA: Don't tell me he's already found one.

ANDERSON: So he says.

JULIA: What is it about these women?

ANDERSON: Don't ask me.

JULIA: Why not ask you? I believe you're familiar with that particular scene.

ANDERSON: Long ago and far away.

JULIA: At least he took her seriously.

ANDERSON: Seriously?

JULIA: An Academy man would have broken the date. For the sake of his career.

ANDERSON: Julia, honey, these Newport types take nothing seriously. They hop on board for a little R and R, and then jump ship to go home and make their pile.

JULIA: He already has a pile, if I've got the right family. They own a whole beer company in Milwaukee.

ANDERSON: I don't give a shit what he owns, as long as he does his job. Now, let's not worry about the kid. *(He downs his drink, takes his glass offstage.)*

JULIA: I'm afraid we have to. For just a tad longer.

ANDERSON: *(From offstage)* Why?

JULIA: I sent him a note, asking him for a drink.

ANDERSON: *(Returning)* When?

JULIA: Tonight.

ANDERSON: For Chrissake, Julia!

JULIA: I had to do *something*, Jim. He left a calling card!

ANDERSON: *(Indicating the card)* Look at the corner!
It means no answer is required.

JULIA: Well, you see, I didn't know that, Jim. I'm not
privy to all these dumb Navy rules. Besides, I know his
family. It won't kill you to have a short drink with one
of your junior officers.

ANDERSON: Except I won't be here.

JULIA: Hey! We have a date tonight.

ANDERSON: Date? Date?

JULIA: The movies at the Officers' Club.

ANDERSON: Oh, God.

JULIA: Remember?

ANDERSON: They've called a joint staff meeting up in
Tokyo.

JULIA: On what?

ANDERSON: Indochina.

JULIA: Don't tell me we're going in *there*.

ANDERSON: *(Checking contents of briefcase)* We're making
contingency plans.

JULIA: We're not even out of Korea.

ANDERSON: This looks like more of the same shit.
Admiral Radford wants to bomb, you know.

JULIA: Bomb who?

ANDERSON: I'm not even sure.

JULIA: What a bunch of blowhards we are!

ANDERSON: I'll convey your opinion to our Task Group.

JULIA: Will you be back tonight?

ANDERSON: First thing tomorrow.

JULIA: Are you sure you don't have some B-girl on the beach?

ANDERSON: Trust me.

JULIA: I shouldn't, but I do. So go to Tokyo. While I struggle through an awkward half-hour with— *(Looks at card)* What does he call himself?

ANDERSON: Sparky. Sparky Watts.

JULIA: I'm sure it's the same one.

ANDERSON: *(A quick kiss)* Have fun. *(He goes.)*

(Clack)

(JULIA stands looking at the calling card.)

READER: Officer here, okusama.

JULIA: Send him in, Noriko.

(Clack)

(Drumming, light change)

(SPARKY comes on, looking resplendently innocent in his dress whites.)

SPARKY: *(Saluting)* Mrs Anderson, I presume.

JULIA: Welcome... Now. Would you mind if I gave you some quick advice, right off the bat?

SPARKY: Shoot.

JULIA: *(Taking his hat)* Never salute a woman. Never wear your hat indoors. And never wear dress whites on unofficial occasions.

SPARKY: Oh, I know all that stuff. I just thought the captain might get a kick if I went whole hog.

JULIA: *(Putting his hat on a stool)* The captain couldn't be here.

SPARKY: Uh-oh. Is he trying to avoid me?

JULIA: Either that, or he's trying to avoid a Communist takeover in Southeast Asia.

SPARKY: I'm not sure he likes me, anyway.

JULIA: He doesn't think you're serious about the Navy.

SPARKY: I am, though. I consider this to be one of the most formative periods in my life.

JULIA: Did you tell him that?

SPARKY: I did.

JULIA: Don't any more.

SPARKY: I hear you.

JULIA: What would you like to drink?

SPARKY: Whatever you're having.

JULIA: A gin and tonic. It's the latest thing.

(A STAGEHAND *enters with two gin and tonics on a tray.)*

JULIA: The British drank it in Singapore to ward off malaria.

SPARKY: How does it do that?

JULIA: The quinine in the tonic. But maybe it's just an excuse to get sauced. *(She hands him a glass, takes one herself.)*

SPARKY: Who needs an excuse?

JULIA: There you go.

(They toast each other.)

JULIA: But now we have to play a short, brisk game of Do-You-Know.

SPARKY: Shoot.

JULIA: I hear you're celebrated throughout the free world as "Sparky" Watts.

SPARKY: I am.

JULIA: And you're also from Milwaukee.

SPARKY: Correct.

JULIA: Do you know a family there named Brandt?
Of Brandt Beer?

SPARKY: My mother was a Brandt.

JULIA: I roomed with Emily Brandt at Westover School.
And again at Smith.

SPARKY: Emily Brandt is my mother's younger sister!

JULIA: We were good friends. I visited her in Milwaukee
before the war. I went to all the dances. She showed me
your family compound on Lake Michigan. It was quite
a spread, I might add.

SPARKY: I'm trying to get away from all that.

JULIA: All that's a lot to get away from.

SPARKY: Yeah, well, out here I'm beyond the pull of
gravity.

JULIA: Emily wrote you were coming to Japan.

SPARKY: I'll bet my mother asked her to.

JULIA: I'll write back that I've tracked you down.

SPARKY: Say hi for me, O K.

JULIA: I'll say I'm keeping an eye on you.

SPARKY: Keeping an eye on me?

JULIA: She asked me to.

SPARKY: Oh, hell. That's just Milwaukee talk,
Mrs Anderson. Just say I'm doing fine.

JULIA: I'd rather say I'm bringing you into the fold.

SPARKY: What fold?

JULIA: This fold. Right here. On the base.

SPARKY: Uh-oh.

JULIA: It's sort of my job, actually, as wife of a senior
officer. I'm supposed to encourage younger officers
to enter in. Do you play bridge?

SPARKY: I'm a passable bridge player.

JULIA: Which means you're good.

SPARKY: Which means I pass.

JULIA: Oh, now, stop. What else do we have?... A sailing group. I got the Navy to ship over six Penguin-class dingies, and we have sailing races every Sunday in Tokyo Bay.

SPARKY: No, thanks.

JULIA: Oh, come on. I imagine you tooted all over Lake Michigan in some Brandt boat.

SPARKY: I get bored on a sailboat, Mrs Anderson.

JULIA: What? A Navy man? Then there's the book club, but I'll bet you're out of our league, being fresh from Princeton. And there's always a tennis tournament of some sort.

SPARKY: I've already entered the singles.

JULIA: Good for you! And we have Sunday softball games. I've worked it so women can play, and it's lots of fun. And there's even a Bible-reading group, which frankly I do NOT recommend.

SPARKY: Halleluiah.

JULIA: How about another drink? You can't fly on one wing, as Jim keeps saying.

(*A* STAGEHAND *brings two more gin and tonics.*)

SPARKY: (*Furtively checking his watch*) Maybe a quick one.

JULIA: (*Taking a glass*) Where did you find her, by the way?

SPARKY: Who?

JULIA: Madame Butterfly.

SPARKY: Oh. We kind of found each other, actually.

JULIA: At the Kit Kat Club?

SPARKY: No.

JULIA: I'm surprised. That's the usual meeting place, isn't it? I hear there's a woman there named Frenchy, who's had her eyes rounded and her breasts built up. Isn't she the one who usually comes up with the girls?

SPARKY: I wouldn't know.

JULIA: Where else, then? The Blue Note? The Cherry Blossom? The Ichi-Ban Numba One Hot Bath and Massage Club?

SPARKY: I didn't meet her at any of those places, Mrs Anderson.

JULIA: Don't be scared of shocking me. I know what goes on.

SPARKY: You sure do.

JULIA: I'm not like those Navy wives who trot endlessly back and forth between the Officers' Club and the P X, never glancing beyond the gate. In fact, I'm not really a Navy wife at all.

SPARKY: Oh?

JULIA: I'm what's known as a Second Wife. I strive to be different.

SPARKY: I can see that.

JULIA: Before I was married, I had a career of my own. I worked for the Voice of America.

SPARKY: Hey. Great.

(They sit side by side on the "couch".)

JULIA: Oh, sure. Two years ago you would have found me in the Philippines, setting up a new radio station. I met Jim when he came steaming into Manila Bay on the *Intrepid*. He was an Air Group Commander and very dashing.

SPARKY: I'll bet he was a wild man.

JULIA: He was not.

SPARKY: Don't kid me. I've seen these carrier pilots hit the beach.

JULIA: He had just lost his only son over North Korea.

SPARKY: Oh. Sorry.

JULIA: Shot down by the Chinese.

SPARKY: Oh boy.

JULIA: Jim was devastated. He had been divorced for years, but now he needed...well, I guess he needed to hear the Voice of America. And there I was, itching for a change. They had just promoted this political hack over my head, and I was fed to the teeth with the flitty State Department bureaucracy. I suppose I could have stayed and fought things out, but....

SPARKY: Shazam! Captain Anderson to the rescue!

JULIA: Well, one thing led to another rather quickly. As can happen in the Far East. As you well know.

SPARKY: I do.

JULIA: So the Navy gave him shore duty, and here we are. *(Pause)* But he can't get over Korea.

SPARKY: Now I know why.

JULIA: You should also know that he's a very nice man. He just wants to be in the air again, or at least at sea. He doesn't like being anchored to a desk.

SPARKY: *(Getting up)* I better go.

JULIA: *(Getting his hat)* Hey, have you seen *From Here to Eternity*?

SPARKY: Damn right. Sinatra's fantastic.

JULIA: Want to see it again? We could have a quick bite first at the Club. I'll introduce you around.

SPARKY: I can't, Mrs Anderson.

JULIA: You're tied up?

SPARKY: I'm tied up.

JULIA: With your newfound friend?

SPARKY: Right.

JULIA: Is she the most attractive thing in the world?

SPARKY: I think so.

JULIA: How can I compete with that?

SPARKY: You don't have to, Mrs Anderson.

JULIA: Your family would want me to. What do I write Emily?

SPARKY: Don't write her anything.

JULIA: I promised I would.

SPARKY: Say I've entered a tennis tournament.

JULIA: I'd like to say I've taken you in tow. *(Thinks)* What if I say you've joined our new dance class?

SPARKY: Dance class?

JULIA: I'm getting the U S O in Tokyo to send us a dance instructor once a week, to teach us all the new steps from the States.

SPARKY: I'm not much of a dancer, Mrs Anderson.

JULIA: One night a week? We need men desperately.

SPARKY: Who would I dance with?

JULIA: There are plenty of pretty girls on this base, Sparky. There's a nurse named Cricket, who's absolutely divine.

SPARKY: I hear she's taken.

JULIA: She is. By that stupid Bible class.

SPARKY: There you are.

JULIA: Because you young officers won't give her the time of day.

SPARKY: I'm taken, too, Mrs Anderson.

JULIA: I won't tell Emily that, if you come to dance class.

SPARKY: Is that a promise?

JULIA: Cross my heart.

SPARKY: One night a week?

JULIA: That's all.

SPARKY: It's a deal.

(*They shake hands.*)

JULIA: I'll write Emily that I found you playing tennis and going to dancing school.

SPARKY: They'll go for that in Milwaukee.

JULIA: And you won't get stuck, I promise.

SPARKY: Thanks for the drink, Mrs Anderson.

JULIA: I can't believe that you haven't seen one woman on this base who is even remotely attractive?

SPARKY: Sure I have.

JULIA: And who, pray tell, would that be?

SPARKY: You, Mrs Anderson.

JULIA: I see you learned to be polite in Milwaukee.

SPARKY: Good night, Mrs Anderson.

(SPARKY *goes.*)

(*Clack*)

READER: Julia? It's Esther! Are you decent?

JULIA: Always. That's my problem.

READER: I just wondered if you're playing bridge tonight.

JULIA: Not tonight, Esther. Tonight I'm seeing *From Here to Eternity.*

READER: By yourself?

JULIA: I'm getting used to that.

READER: It's terribly sexy, Julia. She goes swimming at night with an enlisted man.

JULIA: Sounds like just my meat. *(She goes.)*

(Clack)

(Music. STAGEHANDS *convert the day bed into a barracks bunk as* BOB, *wearing Ensign's bars on his work khakis, comes in, lies down, reads an art book. Also on the bed is a large, official-looking notebook with "TOP SECRET" on the cover.* SPARKY *comes in.* BOB *hides the notebook.)*

SPARKY: You creep.

BOB: I love you, too.

SPARKY: Don't you do anything but sack out?

BOB: Quiet. I'm concentrating.

SPARKY: On what?

BOB: *(Indicates what he is reading)* "The World of Japanese Woodcuts." Hiroshige and his contemporaries.

SPARKY: You should get off your ass occasionally, Bob.

BOB: I'm immersing myself in Japanese culture.

SPARKY: How about immersing yourself in Japanese *life*?

BOB: I'm doing that, too. I met this great guy in Yokohama who's introducing me to all the best art dealers.

SPARKY: So?

BOB: So I'm lining up a set of really good Saito prints at half price.

SPARKY: There's more to Japan than woodcuts, Bob.

BOB: To each his own, pal. I'll study its art, you screw its women.

(As they talk, SPARKY *changes clothes. A* STAGEHAND *takes his whites and hands him a pair of summer slacks, a Hawaiian sport shirt, and loafers.)*

SPARKY: Where do we eat? Here or on the beach?

BOB: I ate already. At the Club.

SPARKY: Up yours.

BOB: I got hungry, for shit's sake.

SPARKY: What was the special?

BOB: Sirloin steak.

SPARKY: Repeat message: up yours.

BOB: Get another hard time from the captain?

SPARKY: He wasn't even there. I talked with his wife.

BOB: Oh hey. Tea and sympathy?

SPARKY: Gin and tonic.

BOB: Was it a drag?

SPARKY: Naaa. She's quite nice, actually. And sexy as hell.

BOB: Did she seduce you?

SPARKY: Naaa.

BOB: You going to seduce her?

SPARKY: She knows my family.

BOB: That's a turnoff.

SPARKY: Yeah.

BOB: Does she know about your girl?

SPARKY: Affirmative. The Captain must've told her.

BOB: She blow a gasket?

SPARKY: Not really.

BOB: They say round-eyed women go ape about the scene ashore.

SPARKY: She's used to it.

BOB: What if it gets back to Milwaukee?

SPARKY: It better not... I'm meeting her later tonight, Bob.

BOB: The Captain's wife?

SPARKY: My girl, dumbbell. Hey, she's got a friend!

BOB: I'm taken, remember?

SPARKY: Oh, right. The girl back home. Ho-hum.

BOB: We're virtually engaged.

SPARKY: You don't talk about her much.

BOB: That's because I'm the strong, silent type.

SPARKY: Yeah, sure.

BOB: Haven't you noticed? I'm Gary Cooper in *High Noon*, cleaning up the world because nobody else will. When all I really want is to go home and marry Grace Kelly.

SPARKY: No, wait. Think big, Bob. Here's who we are. We're Roman centurions, guarding the farflung outposts of the Empire.

BOB: Quo vadis, buddy!

SPARKY: Come on. A simple double date. We'll have a good time.

BOB: I like to screw alone, Sparky.

SPARKY: We do more than screw, Bob.

BOB: Such as?

SPARKY: We walk around.

BOB: You walk around?

SPARKY: And talk.

BOB: Talk. That must be scintillating. Seeing as how you don't speak Japanese and she doesn't speak English.

SPARKY: We get by, Bob.

BOB: *Konbawa. Dozo. Domo arigato. Sayonara.*

SPARKY: We *communicate*, Bob. In a different way. For example, tonight we're going to look at the moon.

BOB: The moon? How original can you get, Sparks.

SPARKY: No, it is. She knows this tearoom which is specially *designed* for you just to sit by this window and watch the July moon rise over this particular pine tree. They have a special word for it. *Tsuki-mi*—moon-viewing. And in the fall, we're going leaf-viewing. And next spring, peony-viewing.

BOB: *Peony*-viewing?

SPARKY: It's a flower, Bob.

BOB: I know that.

SPARKY: Yeah, well, I'm learning to look at things clearly and simply. It's like seeing them for the first time.

BOB: Same with sex?

SPARKY: Damn right! Last night...

BOB: Last night what?

(SPARKY *holds up five fingers.*)

BOB: What? Five times?

SPARKY: I kid you not.

BOB: That's gross, Sparks.

SPARKY: Jealous?

BOB: Of course.

SPARKY: Then come on. You must be horny as a toad. (*He notices the notebook.*) What's this? (*Picks it up*)

BOB: (*Taking it*) Homework.

SPARKY: *Home*work?

BOB: I took the afternoon off to look at prints, so I got behind.

SPARKY: That's the Code Book for Special Operations, Bob.

BOB: And?

SPARKY: Should that be out of Security?

BOB: I'm signed for it.

SPARKY: It's Top Secret, Bob. Your head could roll!

BOB: It's not lost, now is it, Sparks?

SPARKY: Where'd you put it when you went to dinner?

BOB: I took it with me.

SPARKY: You took the Code book to the Officers' Club?

BOB: I put it under my chair.

SPARKY: Jesus, Bob. Top Secret? Under your chair?
I'm amazed you didn't hand it to the hatcheck girl.

BOB: You do your job, Sparks. I'll do mine.

SPARKY: O K. *(Starting out)* Yeah, well. I'm off.

BOB: I'll be up studying this shit when you come in.

SPARKY: I won't be coming in.

BOB: Oh?

SPARKY: She's found an *uchi.*

BOB: A what?

SPARKY: A house. A place to stay.

BOB: You move fast.

SPARKY: It's just a room, actually. No big deal. Tatami
on the floor, futon in the corner. Hot plate in the hall
to whomp up some rice. An outside bath we share with
the mama-san who owns the joint.

BOB: Go slow, Sparks.

SPARKY: I'm not breaking any rules. *(Indicating book)*
Unlike some guys I know.

BOB: Tell that to Milwaukee.

SPARKY: Thank God I don't have to. *(He goes, carrying a
small ditty bag.)*

(BOB exits the other way.)

(Clack)

(ANDERSON *comes on, carrying a document.*)

(STAGEHANDS *remove bed.*)

ANDERSON: *(To* READER*)* Who wrote this, Folsom?

READER: It's signed by Lieutenant Commander Dolan, sir.

ANDERSON: I see who signed it. I asked who wrote it.

READER: I'll find out, sir. *(Clack)* Lieutenant j.g. Watts wrote it, sir.

ANDERSON: Get him.

READER: Aye aye, sir. *(Clack)* Lieutenant j.g. Watts is not at his desk, sir.

ANDERSON: Find out where he is.

READER: Aye aye, sir. *(Clack)* Lieutenant j.g. Watts is on temporary active duty down in Sasebo, sir.

ANDERSON: What's he doing down in Sasebo?

READER: I'll check, sir. *(Clack)* Mr Watts is representing Naval Forces Far East in the Inter-service tennis tournament, sir.

ANDERSON: That goldbricker! *(Pause)* How's he doing?

READER: He has reached the quarter finals, sir.

ANDERSON: Tell him to report to my office when he gets back.

READER: Aye aye, sir. *(Clack)*

(STAGEHANDS *place* ANDERSON's *desk as a larger map of Southeast Asia drops in behind.*)

ANDERSON: Oh, and Folsom?

READER: Sir?

ANDERSON: Where's that model plane I asked for?

READER: I'll check with the Hobby Shop, sir.

ANDERSON: I need something on my desk besides paper, Folsom.

READER: Yes, sir. *(Clack)*

(SPARKY comes on hurriedly, in shirt sleeves.)

SPARKY: Sir?

ANDERSON: Did you win?

SPARKY: Negative, sir.

ANDERSON: Why not?

SPARKY: I lost concentration, sir.

ANDERSON: Too bad. They've scheduled the finals for Hawaii.

SPARKY: Oh, well. I hear Honolulu's just a poor man's Los Angeles, with better beaches.

ANDERSON: There's Pearl Harbor.

SPARKY: I forgot Pearl Harbor, sir.

ANDERSON: Some of us remember it.

SPARKY: I'll stop there on the way home.

ANDERSON: *(Indicating the document)* Do you know what this is, Mr Watts?

SPARKY: It's the report on Haiphong Harbor, sir.

ANDERSON: Your report on Haiphong Harbor.

SPARKY: I wrote some of it.

ANDERSON: It's well written, I'll say that.

SPARKY: Thanks.

ANDERSON: *(Reads)* "Large, verdant bluffs loom over the soupy green water... Beyond the point, white stretches of sand sparkle seductively... On a clear night, the Southern Cross stands out among a great swarm of stars"... Where'd you get this shit?

SPARKY: *Lord Jim*, by Joseph Conrad, sir. In the Officers' Club library.

ANDERSON: That's a novel, Mr Watts.

SPARKY: It is, sir. But Conrad knew his Indochina.

ANDERSON: So you copied from Conrad?

SPARKY: Copied? Negative, sir! I put in lots of my own words.

ANDERSON: I want fewer words, Mr Watts, and more measurements. The width of the harbor, the depth of the water, the accessibility of the shore. Why? So we can put ships in and get people out. *(Hands it to him)* Go clean it up.

SPARKY: *(Taking it)* Yes, sir. *(Starts out)*

ANDERSON: Hold it. I have here another sample of your writing, Mr Watts.

SPARKY: Sir?

ANDERSON: An application attached to a bill of lading.

SPARKY: Oh, that.

ANDERSON: It requests permission for... *(Reads)* "A blue 1955 Chevrolet Bel Air convertible, with wraparound windshield, to be shipped from Oakland, California, to Yokohama, Japan, on the next available transport."

SPARKY: Right, sir.

ANDERSON: You want the Navy to ship you over a new car?

SPARKY: I'm paying for the car, sir.

ANDERSON: When you're in the Harvard Business School, do you want us to ship it back?

SPARKY: Cars are permissible in overseas shore duty, sir. For officers.

ANDERSON: I know the regulations, Watts. I also know that they were designed for married officers domiciled on the beach.

SPARKY: I'm domiciled on the beach, sir.

ANDERSON: With your girl?

SPARKY: She's why I lost the tennis tournament, sir.
I had her on my mind.

ANDERSON: So now you need a car to concentrate.

SPARKY: I need a car for a lot of things, sir.

ANDERSON: Name ten.

SPARKY: Well, for example, this winter we plan to go
skiing up at Shiga Kogen. And we want to climb Fuji
next spring. And some time I want to drive down to
Hiroshima and pay my respects to the dead.

ANDERSON: Hiroshima before Pearl Harbor?

SPARKY: The war is over, sir.

ANDERSON: I hear there've been others.

SPARKY: Cancel the car, sir.

ANDERSON: What?

SPARKY: It's a luxury. I see that now.

ANDERSON: I've already forwarded my approval,
Mr Watts.

SPARKY: Why?

ANDERSON: Because I would have pulled the same
stunt myself. Except I would have made it a red M G.

SPARKY: That would be overdoing it, sir.

ANDERSON: You're a lucky man, Mr Watts.

SPARKY: I recognize that.

ANDERSON: And you're about to get even luckier.

SPARKY: Sir?

ANDERSON: *(Producing another document)* Admiral Stark
is looking for an aide.

SPARKY: An aide?

ANDERSON: His previous one just left for the Hah-vard
B School.

SPARKY: You're kidding, sir.

ANDERSON: I am. But the Admiral likes guys who know the forks. I'm recommending you.

SPARKY: Me?

ANDERSON: You'll have a desk larger than Mussolini's and a signalman second class to answer your phone. You'll enjoy all the pleasures of the peacetime Navy and wear handsome gold aiguillettes while you're doing it.... You seem perplexed, Mr Watts?

SPARKY: I know what these aides do, sir. I've seen them around. They greet congressmen at the airport. They take their wives shopping on the Ginza.

ANDERSON: Yes, but think, Mr Watts. It could lead to an *experience*. You might play golf with William Holden. You might take Miss America out on the town. You might even get reimbursed for using your own car.

SPARKY: I see it as a step back, sir.

ANDERSON: It's a big step forward if you play your cards right. To a first-rate career in Washington when you're mustered out.

SPARKY: It's a step back in *life*, sir. I've already done most of that stuff. Playing golf with my father's friends. Being polite to old ladies. Squiring debs around Milwaukee. It's just country club stuff, sir.

ANDERSON: You mean, like tennis.

SPARKY: I'm shifting to basketball, sir. It's more democratic.

ANDERSON: I see.

SPARKY: I want the real Navy, sir. I want to fix up that harbor report and get it right. I want...oh, hell, I don't know what I want.... *(Indicating Admiral's document)* But I know I don't want that.

ANDERSON: Have you thought about what the Navy might want?

SPARKY: What? *(Pause)* No, I haven't. But I will.

ANDERSON: I would.

SPARKY: But meanwhile I'm asking you not to recommend me.

(Pause)

ANDERSON: I like you, Watts. I don't know why, but I do. You're wet behind the ears, you think it's one big game, but I kind of like having you around.

SPARKY: Thank you, sir.

ANDERSON: I've got to submit a flight plan for a trip to Saigon next month. Want to tag along?

SPARKY: Affirmative.

ANDERSON: We'll go by way of Manila and Hong Kong.

SPARKY: Sounds great.

ANDERSON: We'll fly over Haiphong Harbor, so you can improve on your Joseph Conrad.

SPARKY: I'm with you all the way!

(ANDERSON goes off.)

(Clack)

(Music: a popular cha-cha from the fifties)

(JULIA comes on, waving to "others." She puts her purse down somewhere. A STAGEHAND assists SPARKY in putting on his jacket.)

READER: *(As dance instructor)* Join the line with the others, please, sir. Facing front. Now follow directions, please.

(SPARKY stands as if in a line.)

JULIA: *(As if to bystanders)* Hi, everybody, sorry I'm late. Come on, Cricket. Come on, Esther.

READER: Step, step, one two three.

(SPARKY *awkwardly tries to dance.*)

JULIA: *(Seeing* SPARKY) Well, well. Look who showed up.

SPARKY: That was the deal.

JULIA: It was indeed. *(She joins him in the "line".)*

READER: And cha cha cha.

SPARKY: *(As they learn the dance)* I hope you've kept your end of the bargain.

JULIA: I have, I have.

SPARKY: I guess I'd hear soon enough if you hadn't.

READER: Side step. One, two, three.

JULIA: Now admit it. Isn't it fun to be back in your own element?

SPARKY: No offense, Mrs Anderson, but I consider this sort of a duty dance.

JULIA: Don't you like hearing the songs from home?

SPARKY: Sort of.

JULIA: Of course you do. *(Trying to accommodate the cha-cha rhythm)* "Breathes there a man with soul so dead who never to himself has said, This is my own, my native land...."

READER: Cha cha cha.

JULIA: You'll be the life of the party when you get home.

SPARKY: Oh, sure.

JULIA: You'll know all the new steps. The girls will be falling at your feet.

SPARKY: Big deal.

READER: Step forward.

JULIA: They'll wonder how you learned, way out in the Far East.

SPARKY: I'll say it was my duty as an officer and a gentleman.

JULIA: Here's what you'll say... You'll say that during your wanderings in the land of Oz, you met Glinda the Good, who pointed you home.

SPARKY: I won't be here for the third session, by the way.

JULIA: I know. You're taking a trip with my husband, you lucky duck.

SPARKY: I like him.

JULIA: So do I. He says you've had a car shipped over.

SPARKY: I'm touring the countryside.

JULIA: I'd love to do that.

SPARKY: *(Stopping his dancing)* Why don't you? You stay at these weird, wonderful country inns. You sit and soak in these great hot baths.

JULIA: Sounds dreamy.

SPARKY: Grab your husband and a car from the motor pool and shove off.

JULIA: It's not that easy, Sparky.

SPARKY: Come on. He's a full-fledged Captain in the regular Navy.

JULIA: That's why it's not that easy.

READER: *(The music stops.)* All right, people. Select a partner, please, and we'll try it again as couples.

JULIA: Go ask some girl.

SPARKY: Can I choose whoever I want?

JULIA: Of course you can.

SPARKY: *(Bowing)* Then I choose you.

JULIA: That's taking the easy way out.

SPARKY: Maybe. Maybe not.

READER: Now let's try to put it all together.

(Different, quieter cha-cha music this time. SPARKY *and* JULIA *dance together.)*

JULIA: The next dance, I insist you ask somebody else.

SPARKY: Why?

JULIA: So I can write Emily that I've lured you out of the fleshpots of Asia into the arms of a nice American girl.

SPARKY: *(Pulling away)* Hey! I thought you weren't going to tell.

JULIA: I was just kidding, Sparky.

SPARKY: Thank God.

(They do a more complicated step.)

JULIA: You're good, by the way.

SPARKY: I stink.

JULIA: No, seriously. You move very well.

SPARKY: Depends who I'm with.

JULIA: I think maybe we've had enough cha-cha for one night.

(She gives the "cut" sign to the music. The music ends. SPARKY *and* JULIA *clap.)*

READER: Very good, people... Now we will have a free dance.

(A slow tune: popular and danceable)

SPARKY: I love this song. *(He turns to dance with her again.)*

JULIA: Oh no you don't. *(Indicating)* Go ask that girl in blue standing by the punch bowl. Her name is Betsy, and she's cute as a button.

SPARKY: *(Looking)* No she isn't.

JULIA: She could be. If someone danced with her.

SPARKY: I'm the shy type.

JULIA: Hardly. Now go on. I should circulate.

SPARKY: *(Holding out his arms)* One more dance. Please.

JULIA: All right, but very briefly.

(They dance, using the whole stage.)

SPARKY: This is easy.

JULIA: You make it easy. You know how to lead.

SPARKY: My fitness report says I've got leadership qualities.

JULIA: No, I'm serious. You're good.

SPARKY: So are you, Mrs Anderson.

JULIA: Call me Julia. I won't feel so ancient.

SPARKY: The skipper's wife? Better not.

JULIA: At least while we're dancing.

SPARKY: O K, Julia.

(They dance closer.)

SPARKY: Is the Captain a good dancer?

JULIA: Not with me. We always want to go in different directions.

SPARKY: That's deadly when you're dancing. The man should be boss. *(He leads her into a fancy turn.)*

JULIA: So I see... I'll bet you learned that in dancing school.

SPARKY: I can only turn clockwise.

JULIA: Clockwise is fine by me.

(They turn again.)

JULIA: What about your little friend?

SPARKY: What about her?

JULIA: Can she dance?

SPARKY: Sure.

JULIA: She can?

SPARKY: She loves dancing.

JULIA: Western dancing? This kind of dancing?

SPARKY: We go dancing a lot.

JULIA: Do you mean to tell me that if you took her to the Milwaukee Mid-Winter Country Club dance, she'd feel right in the swim?

SPARKY: On the dance floor she would.

JULIA: You're pulling my leg.

SPARKY: I'll show you, if you want.

JULIA: How can you possibly show me?

SPARKY: I'll dance with her right now.

(JULIA *breaks away.*)

JULIA: She's here?

SPARKY: Sure.

JULIA: Where?

SPARKY: *(Indicating)* Over there. Serving the punch.

JULIA: *(Looking)* That waitress?

SPARKY: That's her.

JULIA: Your girlfriend is a waitress here at the Officers' Club?

SPARKY: That's how we met. She served me dinner the night I arrived. One thing led to another.

JULIA: I didn't know that.

SPARKY: Shall I ask her to dance?

JULIA: I wouldn't.

SPARKY: Why not?

JULIA: For one thing, she's wearing her uniform.

SPARKY: So am I.

JULIA: She wouldn't do it anyway.

SPARKY: She would if the Captain's wife said O K.

JULIA: Well, the Captain's wife says *not* O K.

SPARKY: *(Starting off)* Let me show you our Gene Kelly number.

JULIA: I said no!

SPARKY: *(Returning)* Just kidding. The way you were.

JULIA: Very funny.

SPARKY: She's great looking, though, isn't she?

JULIA: She's very pretty.

SPARKY: I think she's beautiful.

JULIA: She's exotic, I'll say that.

SPARKY: Want to meet her? I'll introduce you.

JULIA: She looks very busy, Sparky.

SPARKY: *(Taking her arm)* Come on. Just say hello. Her English is amazing.

JULIA: *(Breaking away)* Sparky, NO! I don't intend to do that. No. The rules are very clear about this, Sparky. There is to be no fraternization between officers and the indigenous staff.

SPARKY: During working hours.

JULIA: She's working now.

SPARKY: I'm not.

JULIA: You're not funny, Sparky, so just stop this right now. This really throws me off, frankly.

SPARKY: Are you prejudiced?

JULIA: Of course not.

SPARKY: I think you're prejudiced against the Japanese.

JULIA: Maybe you'd better go, Sparky.

SPARKY: Fair enough. Am I still in the class?

JULIA: Not if she's here.

SPARKY: This is her job.

JULIA: I'd advise her to do something else.

SPARKY: She gets overtime here.

JULIA: I don't care what she gets, Sparky. I don't think it's fair for you to be trotting people around the dance floor, while you're making eyes at some little Jap waitress over their shoulder.

SPARKY: I didn't make eyes at—

JULIA: I'd prefer not to argue about it, Sparky. Now please go.

SPARKY: Are you breaking our deal?

JULIA: I don't know, Sparky. I really don't. I find this very upsetting.

SPARKY: O K. Write home, if you want.

JULIA: I didn't say I'd do that, Sparky.

SPARKY: Know what? I hope you do! Tell them I'm not in love with some whore from the Kit Kat Club.

JULIA: In *love*? In *love* with?

SPARKY: Actually I am. I think I am, Julia.

JULIA: The name is Mrs Anderson, Sparky. And from here on in, I think we might both pay a little more attention to the rules!

(She goes off. SPARKY looks after her, looks off at his girl, then strides off another way.)

(Clack)

(Rain sounds; gloomy lighting)

(STAGEHAND crosses rattling a rainstick)

(BOB comes on in uniform and raincoat with hat covering, duffle bag slung over his shoulder, carrying several slips of paper. A STAGEHAND stands by him.)

BOB: Request permission for ten days' emergency leave.

READER: Destination?

BOB: Enid, Oklahoma.

READER: Purpose of visit?

BOB: My father's dying.

READER: Red Cross verification?

BOB: *(Handing* STAGEHAND *a document)* Here.

READER: Means of transportation?

BOB: *(Handing over another document)* Military Air. Priority Second Class.

READER: Replacement?

BOB: Lieutenant j.g. Wallace Watts.

READER: Watts cleared for Top Secret?

BOB: Affirmative.

READER: Leave granted. *(Clack)*

(More rain sounds)

(SPARKY, wearing a raincoat and hat-covering joins him. They walk as STAGEHANDS set up a table behind with a large loose-leaf notebook on it.)

SPARKY: Sorry about your old man, buddy.

BOB: He's the reason I'm in the Navy. Made me join R O T C at college. Said it would toughen me up. At least I can say goodbye to him in uniform.

SPARKY: And see your girl in the process.

BOB: Right. Here's the stuff.

(They go to the table. Lights suggest an interior.)

SPARKY: *(Looking at notebook)* Is this all?

BOB: Joe Melnick is taking over Secret and Confidential.

SPARKY: I get hit with Top Secret?

BOB: I didn't think Joe would want the responsibility.

SPARKY: Think I do?

BOB: I think you're a good friend.

SPARKY: I can only do it for ten days, Bob. I'm doing a flyover with the skipper on the 21st.

BOB: I'll be back by then... Sign at the bottom of this cover sheet.

SPARKY: Better check things over first.

BOB: How gung ho can you get?

SPARKY: I should know what I'm sitting on, Bob.

(SPARKY starts checking the material. BOB watches.)

(More rain sounds)

(ANDERSON crosses upstage, followed by JULIA; he wears raingear; she carries a Japanese umbrella.)

JULIA: I heard there's a staff job available in Tokyo. You could send him up there.

ANDERSON: That job's long gone.

JULIA: Then throw him onto some ship for a while.

ANDERSON: He wants to be here, Julia.

JULIA: He doesn't know what he wants.

ANDERSON: *(Stopping)* Why do you care so much?

JULIA: I promised Emily.

ANDERSON: Who's Emily? God?

JULIA: She's a friend.

ANDERSON: You haven't seen her for years.

JULIA: She is my best friend, Jim!

ANDERSON: Oh, really? Then tell her the kid's doing fine.

JULIA: He needs guidance, Jim. And you're not helping.

ANDERSON: Who am I? Some camp counselor?

JULIA: You have a responsibility not to let him mess up his life.

ANDERSON: Know what I think, Julia?

JULIA: What do you think, Jim?

ANDERSON: I think we talk about him too much. Matter of fact, I need to get his orders cut for our trip. *(He goes.)*

JULIA: *(Following)* At least you'll be getting him *away*... Jim? I'm talking to you, Jim! *(She goes off.)*

BOB: *(Watching* SPARKY *go over the documents)* I appreciate this, by the way.

SPARKY: That's O K. *(Takes up the TOP SECRET notebook)* Code book. *(Checks cover sheet)* Eighty-seven pages. *(Checks the pages in notebook)* Eighty-seven. Right. *(Jokingly)* You didn't lose any at the Officer's Club.

BOB: No, I didn't.

SPARKY: *(Checking the next documents)* Electronic countermeasures, thirty-eighth parallel...eighteen pages. Right. *(Reviewing another document)* Hey. What's this?

BOB: What?

SPARKY: *(Reading)* MAG Vietnam.

BOB: MAG means Military Advisory Group.

SPARKY: Yeah, but Vietnam?

BOB: That's what we're calling French Indochina now. Vietnam, North and South. They're through with the French and don't like China, so they want their own name.

SPARKY: *(Reading)* This says we've got men in the South.

BOB: Just military advisors.

SPARKY: I thought Eisenhower said we were staying out.

BOB: That's why it's Top Secret.

SPARKY: Oh. *(He continues ckecking documents.)*

BOB: *(Watching him)* There's a lot of Top Secret stuff on Vietnam. French stuff, Chinese stuff, Cambodian stuff....

SPARKY: *(He interrupts, looking at a document.)* This is wrong.

BOB: What is wrong?

SPARKY: *(Indicating cover sheet)* It says there are three copies of this. I only see two. *(Reads cover of top copy)* First of three copies. *(Reads cover of third)* Third of three copies... Where's the second?

BOB: Out at the moment.

SPARKY: Where's the signature for it?

BOB: What?

SPARKY: Who signed for copy number two?

BOB: I can't say.

SPARKY: You can't *say*? Why can't you say?

BOB: Because...because it's Top Secret.

SPARKY: That's a circular argument, Bob.

BOB: Don't worry about it, Sparks.

SPARKY: Don't *worry* about it? Of course I worry about it. I'm signing for something that isn't here!

BOB: I know exactly where the document is, Sparky.

SPARKY: Where?

BOB: I'm not at liberty to tell you.

SPARKY: Have you lost it, Bob?

BOB: I haven't lost it.

SPARKY: A signature should be here, man.

BOB: I know that.

SPARKY: Is this why you didn't give this stuff to Melnick?

BOB: He's an Academy man.

SPARKY: You thought I wouldn't be such a stickler?

BOB: I thought you were a friend.

SPARKY: Friends don't pull fast ones on each other, Bob.

BOB: *(Checking watch)* I've got to get to the airport.

SPARKY: I have to know where every document is, Bob.

BOB: O K. *(Pause)* It's with a civilian. *(Pause)* Which is why he didn't sign.

SPARKY: Civilians can sign—if they have clearance.

BOB: This one's Japanese, Sparky.

SPARKY: Japanese?

BOB: Right.

SPARKY: You gave a Top Secret document to a Japanese civilian?

BOB: I had to, Sparky.

SPARKY: Why did you have to?

BOB: Because... *(Pause)* Oh, shit. *(Pause)* Because he had pictures, Sparky.

SPARKY: Pictures?

BOB: Photographs.

SPARKY: Of what, for Chrissake?

BOB: Of me. *(Pause)* And him. *(Pause)* Together.

SPARKY: Say again.

BOB: I shacked up with him, Sparky.

SPARKY: What about your girl?

BOB: I made her up.

SPARKY: You mean, you're a...

BOB: Homosexual, Sparks. That's what I am.

SPARKY: Jesus, Bob. Who's the guy?

BOB: The guy who set me up with the woodcuts.

SPARKY: The arty guy?

BOB: Right.

SPARKY: You gave him a Top Secret document?

BOB: He swore he'd return it. Then this telegram came about Dad.

SPARKY: Is he a Communist?

BOB: He's a son of a bitch is what he is!

SPARKY: He's a Communist spy, Bob. He's probably showing it to the Russians right now.

BOB: All I know is I hate the bastard. I'd like to kill him.

READER: Excuse me, sir. Carpool calling. Transportation ready and waiting.

SPARKY: *(To* READER*)* Another minute, Martin. *(To* BOB*)* This is very bad, Bobby. You are in very, very hot water here.

BOB: It's not codes or anything, Sparky. Nothing significant.

SPARKY: *(Looks at copy)* Nothing significant? I see names here. There are *people* involved. *(Reads)* It says these are guys...from the South Vietnamese Special Forces...who have infiltrated into the North.

BOB: They classify all sorts of junk, Sparky. You know that. Anything they don't know they stamp Top Secret.

SPARKY: Did you get your pictures back?

BOB: Yes.

SPARKY: The negatives, too?

BOB: No. Not yet.

SPARKY: They could put the *squeeze* on you. Bob! For other stuff.

BOB: Oh, Jesus.

SPARKY: You've got to think about this, Bob. I've got to, too. *(He stands, thinking.)*

(More drumbeats)

*(*JULIA *comes on with a writing folder. She sits on a stool, opens folder, writes.)*

JULIA: Dear Emily... *(She sits pondering, pen poised.)*

BOB: Give me a break, Sparks.

SPARKY: I can't sign for this stuff.

BOB: Oh, come on.

SPARKY: It would be a lie if I signed for stuff that's not here.

BOB: Since when are you George Washington?

SPARKY: I've done lots of crap. But I can't do this.

BOB: O K. Don't sign then. Who's going to check? I'll be back in ten days, and retrieve the document, and that's that.

SPARKY: *(Indicating paper)* Meanwhile guys could get caught and killed, Bob!

BOB: So what do I do, then? What do you want me to do?

SPARKY: I don't know.

(They look at each other.)

*(*ANDERSON *comes on elsewhere. A* STAGEHAND *brings him a model of a Corsair fighter plane.)*

READER: The hobby shop sent this over, sir, with apologies for the delay.

*(*ANDERSON *takes the model, looks at it lovingly.)*

ANDERSON: Tell 'em thanks. Better yet, I'll send a memo.

READER: Yes, sir.

*(*ANDERSON *stands, admiring the model.* JULIA *begins to write determinedly.)*

SPARKY: You've got to tell the Captain about this, Bob.

BOB: It'll all come *out!*

SPARKY: You've got to do it.

BOB: I'd be court-martialed!

SPARKY: Which is worse? That, or getting guys killed.

READER: Excuse me, sir. Carpool calling again.

BOB: *(Grabbing his bag and starting out)* I'm going.

SPARKY: *I'll* have to tell him then, Bob.

BOB: Sparky.

SPARKY: I'll have to. It's my job. I'm a Naval officer.

BOB: Oh, come on! You're just temporary out of Newport!

SPARKY: I took an oath, Bob! So did you!

(Pause)

BOB: Jesus, I hate the Navy.

SPARKY: I don't.

BOB: To you it's one big adventure.

SPARKY: This is no adventure, Bob. Turning in a friend. This is shit, if you want to know.

BOB: Then don't do it.

SPARKY: I wouldn't have to if you did it yourself.

(Pause)

BOB: *(Grimly)* You win, Lieutenant Watts. *(Calls off)* Martin! Cancel my transportation.

SPARKY: The Captain's a good guy, Bob. He might go easy on you.

BOB: Fat chance. *(He gathers up the documents from the desk.)*

SPARKY: I can't lie, Bob. I can't live with that.

BOB: Looks like I can't either.

(He goes, carrying duffle bag and Top Secret material. SPARKY *looks after him.)*

ANDERSON: *(Goes to desk, dictates)* Memo. To: Hobby Shop Personnel. From: Me. Message: Thanks, guys, for the model of my best girl. She'll help keep me sane. Respectfully, et cetera.

(He lands the plane on the desk as if it were an aircraft carrier.)

*(*JULIA *reads what she has written.)*

JULIA: Dear Emily. I hate to rock the boat, but I think you should know that your dear nephew is somewhat involved with a Japanese lady. I wouldn't bother to write except that here in the Far East these things can become rather serious rather quickly....

*(*BOB *enters* ANDERSON's *"office.")*

BOB: May I speak to you, sir?

*(*ANDERSON *looks up.)*

*(*JULIA *silently works on her letter.)*

*(*SPARKY *looks on, as if from the outside.)*

(Drum beats from the DRUMMER*)*

(Clack from READER*)*

(Blackout)

END OF ACT ONE

ACT TWO

(At rise)

(A garish, Frenchy screen or drop. The stage has been preset with a high table to serve as a "bar".)

(READER enters, takes her position. ANDERSON enters with an almost empty beer glass, sits at the bar.)

(Clack and drumbeats)

READER: A bar in Saigon. *(Clack)*

(Music: another popular song from the period)

(ANDERSON drinks his beer.)

READER: You want numba one Saigon girl, Okey Dokey?

ANDERSON: No thanks, Buddy.

READER: Special price for American G I officer, Okey Dokey?

ANDERSON: Just bring me another beer, Okey Dokey?

(SPARKY comes on, carrying a silk scarf.)

SPARKY: Look what I got on the street.

ANDERSON: For your girl?

SPARKY: Who else?

ANDERSON: Nice.

(STAGEHAND brings two full beers.)

(SPARKY shakes out the scarf.)

SPARKY: Made in France. They're having a clearance sale.

ANDERSON: I'll bet.

SPARKY: Want to get one for your wife?

ANDERSON: Christ, I forgot.

SPARKY: Want me to go get her one?

ANDERSON: I'll pick up perfume at the airport. What's that brand she likes? *Joy*? Is it *Joy*?

SPARKY: How would I know?

ANDERSON: I think she likes *Joy*.

SPARKY: They're putting in a Kit Kat Club down the street.

ANDERSON: That used to be a French Restaurant.

SPARKY: Guess we're taking over, huh?

ANDERSON: Looks that way.

SPARKY: Guess we have to, right? I mean, if Vietnam goes, Thailand goes, right? What do you think?

ANDERSON: What do I think? I think there are lots of guys sitting around Washington who went to the right schools, and took the right courses, and learned a lot of simple-minded shit about domino theories and power vacuums and spheres of influence, and now they're playing games all over the world. *(Pointedly)* I believe you know the type.

SPARKY: Maybe I do, but I'm not one of them.

ANDERSON: Trouble is, these games are for real. Guys *die* in these games. So they're careful never to draft their own sons.

SPARKY: Yeah.

ANDERSON: Oh, hell, no more politics. On this trip, I'm just an old flyboy testing his wings.

SPARKY: You sure are.

ANDERSON: How about that, huh? Our little side excursion over the Tonkin Gulf?

SPARKY: I never thought I'd be landing on a carrier. It's like coming in on a postage stamp.

ANDERSON: A postage stamp that's going thirty knots: and bouncing up and down!

SPARKY: Know what? When they waved us in, and the tail-hook caught, I—never mind.

ANDERSON: Tell Daddy.

SPARKY: I got a slight hard-on.

ANDERSON: *(Raising his glass)* Welcome to the club.

SPARKY: It *is* a club, too! All those guys in colored jerseys scampering around on deck! Like the squires serving the knights in *Ivanhoe*. Did you notice they gave you a hand when you opened the cockpit?

ANDERSON: They know me. I skippered an air group on that ship in forty-five.

SPARKY: So they said.

ANDERSON: We devised an attack pattern for when the kamikazes came in. *(Demonstrating with his hands)* We'd get on their tail, see? One high, one low, like this. Then switch. Like this. They wrote it up in *Life* magazine. Drew diagrams and everything. Called it the Anderson weave.

SPARKY: I'll look it up when we get back.

ANDERSON: *Life* won't tell you how many guys we lost. They never write that.

SPARKY: Yeah.

ANDERSON: But flying's in my blood... In Teddy's, too. *(Pause)* Ted was my son. Killed up by the Yalu River.

SPARKY: I know.

ANDERSON: Who told you?

SPARKY: Your wife.

ANDERSON: I can't get over it. She tell you that?

SPARKY: She did.

ANDERSON: I thought maybe with a new wife, and shore duty, I'd be able to switch gears.... But I sit at that desk, pushing papers around, and think.... *(Pause)* I think too much. *(Pause)* I've applied for sea duty again. Don't tell Julia.

SPARKY: I never would.

ANDERSON: Ever thought of staying in?

SPARKY: Me?

ANDERSON: You're an asshole, but you're a Navy asshole.

SPARKY: Thanks a bunch.

ANDERSON: You'd have to become a flyer, though. To get ahead. But you've got the makings of one. The car, the babe on the beach, the hard-on.

SPARKY: Yeah, well...

ANDERSON: I'll recommend you for flight school.

SPARKY: Let me think about that.

ANDERSON: Please do.

READER: Young officer want nice Vietnamese girl?

SPARKY: No, thanks.

READER: Fuckie-fuckie, suckie-suckie...

ANDERSON: *(Getting up, going to "door")* Scram, guy! *(To* SPARKY*)* Still monogamous?

SPARKY: Absolutely.

ANDERSON: Let me tell you something. May I tell you something?

SPARKY: Sure.

ANDERSON: Remember I had to go to that special briefing when we were in Manila?

SPARKY: Sure.

ANDERSON: I didn't.

SPARKY: You didn't go?

ANDERSON: I went to visit a friend instead.

SPARKY: A friend?

ANDERSON: A Filipino girl. I wanted to see how she was doing. But she had gone home.

SPARKY: Oh.

ANDERSON: I used to live with her. Whenever we came into port, I'd head straight for that girl. I was nuts about her, in some ways. But then Teddy was killed, and suddenly I needed...I wanted...I met Julia. When the chips are down, you gravitate to your own kind.

SPARKY: You think?

ANDERSON: She's the Voice of America, Sparky. She keeps us in line.

SPARKY: She tries.

ANDERSON: She wrote your folks, you know. About your girl.

SPARKY: Shit. Knew it.

ANDERSON: You haven't heard back?

SPARKY: I'm sure I will.

ANDERSON: She saw it as her obligation.

SPARKY: That's O K, Jim. I can handle it. I'm a big boy now.

ANDERSON: (Looks at watch) Well. Back to the paper empire. (Standing up) Now the fun's over, I can tell you this: I'm convening a special court-martial on your friend.

SPARKY: Oh no.

ANDERSON: I'm required to. I got a cable from the investigating officer.

SPARKY: But he turned himself in.

ANDERSON: That's in his favor. Other things aren't. You know the other things?

SPARKY: He told me.

ANDERSON: This will be a tough one.

SPARKY: I feel shitty about it.

ANDERSON: Why? Because you flagged the guy? I'm putting a commendation in your fitness report.

SPARKY: That makes me feel worse.

ANDERSON: I'm telling you, kid, go to flight school. Get on a carrier. It all shakes down at sea.

SPARKY: Why?

ANDERSON: For one thing, there's no sex.

SPARKY: You hope.

ANDERSON: Go fuck yourself.

(They go.)

(Clack)

(Drumbeats as BOB *comes on)*

READER: Hiya, Bob. May I call you Bob?

BOB: O K.

READER: Sit down, Bob.

BOB: Thanks. *(He sits on a stool.)*

READER: They've assigned me to be your defense council.

BOB: I know.

READER: So call me Hank.

BOB: O K, Hank.

READER: I'm not a lawyer, Bob, but I took pre-law at Penn, along with R O T C.

BOB: I see.

READER: And I'm headed for Law School when I get out. I'm already accepted at Columbia.

BOB: Congratulations.

READER: Thanks. So. They treating you O K, Bob?

BOB: They've moved me out of the B O Q. I'm under house arrest in the V I P wing.

READER: Hey, take advantage. Listen to the Army-McCarthy hearings on short wave. Enjoy the food.

BOB: I'll try.

READER: O K, now, here's the thing. I propose we plead guilty at the top and go for mitigating circumstances.

BOB: What do you mean?

READER: Point one: You turned yourself in. That was brave, Bob. I'll emphasize that.

BOB: O K.

READER: Point two: the Top Secret stuff turned out to be wrong.

BOB: Wrong?

READER: Those names, Bob. It turns out that three out of those four South Vietnamese infiltrators were already working for the North.

BOB: What about the fourth?

READER: I'm afraid you exposed him, Bob. He was caught and killed by the Viet Cong.

BOB: Oh, God.

READER: Now, calm down. You've got other things going for you, Bob.

BOB: What other things?

READER: Your Dad's heart attack. That caused emotional distress and confusion. Which is what I told your mom.

BOB: My mom?

READER: I called her long distance, Bob. Felt I had to.

BOB: What else did you tell her?

READER: Everything, Bob.

BOB: Why?

READER: I thought she might have something to add.

BOB: Did she?

READER: I'm afraid she hung up on me, Bob.

BOB: Oh, God.

READER: No, now wait, kid. The homosexual thing might save your ass in the long run. The Navy won't want it known that their Top Secret Control Officer at a major naval base in the Far East turned out to be a fruit. My bet is they'll sweep you under the rug.

BOB: Under the rug...

READER: I'm pretty sure, Bob. But hey, I've got to get back to work. I get such a kick out of this legal stuff that I forget it's just a collateral duty.

BOB: Thank you, sir.

READER: Hank, Bob. Remember? We're both Navy officers, after all.

BOB: Thank you, Hank. *(He goes.)*

(Clack)

(JULIA comes on, carrying a stack of mail.)

JULIA: *(Tapping a "bell"; as if to a store clerk)* Excuse me. I wonder if you have a size forty dark green cashmere cardigan sweater from Hong Kong sitting around somewhere. I ordered it through the P X.

READER: I'll check in back, ma'am.

(JULIA waits. SPARKY comes on.)

JULIA: *(Seeing him)* Well, hello.

SPARKY: Mrs Anderson.

JULIA: I suppose you're furious at me.

SPARKY: Why?

JULIA: For writing your family.

SPARKY: Oh, that.

JULIA: Didn't they explode?

SPARKY: I just got a long letter from my mother, and she never mentioned it.

JULIA: Don't tell me they don't care?

SPARKY: Sure they care. This is what's known in my family as the lull before the storm.

JULIA: Let's hope it's not a typhoon.

SPARKY: Whatever it is, it's their problem, not mine.

(Pause)

JULIA: What brings you to the P X, Sparky Watts?

SPARKY: I'm looking for a birthday present.

JULIA: For guess who?

SPARKY: I already got her one of those new G E self-timing rice makers, but I'm not sure it's enough.

JULIA: You want something more personal.

SPARKY: Right.

(A STAGEHAND *brings on a sweater in a box.)*

READER: I found your sweater, Mrs Captain-san.

JULIA: Thank you. *(She opens the box, takes a look.)*

SPARKY: *(Looking)* Nice sweater.

JULIA: If it fits. *(She starts out.)*

SPARKY: Try it on.

JULIA: Here?

SPARKY: Why not?

JULIA: Well, all right. *(She puts on sweater.)*

SPARKY: You look great in that.

JULIA: Do I?

SPARKY: You remind me of this girl I met after the Dartmouth game at the Cottage Club. She was from Vassar and wore a sweater just like that.

JULIA: Oh? *(As if to salesclerk)* I might as well wear it home, Miss. Charge my account.

READER: Yes, Mrs Captain-San.

JULIA: *(Leaving the P X)* Goodbye, Sparky.

SPARKY: See you at the Cottage Club sometime, Mrs Anderson.

JULIA: I'm a Smith girl, Sparky, and strongly opposed to the Club system. *(She remains upstage, sorting through her mail.)*

SPARKY: *(As if to clerk)* I want to buy one of those. Same color, everything. Except smaller.

(Clack)

(He goes.)

(JULIA *comes downstage, sits, reads a letter.)*

JULIA: *(Reading aloud)* Dear Julia.
Forgive the delay, but after your letter, we decided to call a major family confab. You can imagine how shocked we all were. Sparky's mother kept bursting into tears, and old Granny Brandt spilled her cocktail right down her front. We can live with the waitress thing. Billy Schmidt just married his dental hygenist, and we all fell into line. But *Japanese*! From the country that bombed Pearl Harbor! That's the last straw. Now, Sparky can be stubborn as a mule, so we're all pretending we don't know or care. But rest assured, major steps are being taken! You and I will be giggling about this whole situation at our next Smith reunion.

Which will be what? Our twentieth! Eeek! *Tempus fugit.*
Meanwhile, thanks loads for blowing the whistle. Love,
Emily.

(JULIA *folds the letter and puts it in her pocket and remains
onstage.)*

(Clack)

(Lights change.)

(A STAGEHAND *comes on with* ANDERSON, *in golfing
clothes.)*

*(*STAGEHAND *hands him a "golf club". It should simply be
the handle.* ANDERSON *places a "ball," addresses it, and
swings. The* DRUMMER *makes the sound of a club hitting
a ball.* ANDERSON *watches his drive admiringly.)*

READER: Numba one drive, Captain-san.

ANDERSON: *(Calling to* JULIA*)* You're up, babe!

*(*JULIA *gets up. A* STAGEHAND *hands her a "club".
She places the "ball", addresses it and swings.)*

JULIA: Rats! Right into the pond!

ANDERSON: That used to be a bomb crater.

JULIA: Oh, yes?

ANDERSON: This whole course was made by the
Sea-Bees in three weeks out of a few old rice paddies.
Now the Japs want it back.

JULIA: So they can grow rice?

ANDERSON: So they can play golf.... Take another drive.
(He places her "ball".)

JULIA: What am I doing wrong?

ANDERSON: You have no follow-through.

JULIA: Story of my life.

ANDERSON: Let me show you. *(He stands behind her,
arms around her, puts his hands over her hands.)* Loosen
your grip.

JULIA: I didn't know golf could be so sexy.

ANDERSON: *(Standing back)* Now, turn your shoulders and really follow through.

(She swings, a pop from the DRUMMER, *she looks out, groans.)*

ANDERSON: Now you're trying to kill it.

JULIA: Maybe I'm sore about something.

ANDERSON: Sore?

JULIA: I hear you stopped at Manila on your way to Saigon.

ANDERSON: Who told you that?

JULIA: Mary Leahy's husband made up the flight plan.

ANDERSON: Ah, the Navy.

JULIA: Why did you stop there?

ANDERSON: Official business.

JULIA: Did you see her?

ANDERSON: No. *(Pause)* She wasn't there.

JULIA: You looked her up?

ANDERSON: To see how she was doing.

JULIA: Oh, sure.

ANDERSON: She's back with her folks, Julia. That's that.

JULIA: All right, Jim. All right.

ANDERSON: *(To* STAGEHANDS*)* You guys go on ahead, O K?

(The STAGEHANDS *exit.)*

ANDERSON: Now I've got one for you, Julia.

JULIA: Shoot.

ANDERSON: About your correspondence with your Milwaukee pen pal.

JULIA: We've been through all that.

ANDERSON: I just received a cable from Washington.

JULIA: Washington?

ANDERSON: Some congressman from Wisconsin is getting into the act.

JULIA: You can't be serious.

ANDERSON: Your friends at Brandt Beer seem to have pulled a few strings.

JULIA: Why a congressman?

ANDERSON: To make me send him home.
(Takes the cable from his pocket, shows it to her)

JULIA: *(Taking the cable)* What? When?

ANDERSON: Immediately. Just because he's having a—what do the Australians call it? A walkabout. The kid's having a little walkabout in Japan.

JULIA: He did say he *loved* her, Jim.

ANDERSON: They all say that. At one time or another.

JULIA: The voice of experience.

ANDERSON: These things burn themselves out.

JULIA: Do they, Jim?

ANDERSON: I haven't seen her once since I met you. Knock it off, Julia! Now how do I deal with that lousy congressman!

(He goes off. JULIA stands looking at the cablegram.)

(Clack)

(Lights change.)

(Clack)

JULIA: *(Calling off)* You're here on the edge of the green, Jim.

(ANDERSON comes on, eyes his ball.)

ANDERSON: Christ, what a lousy lie.

JULIA: *(Putting; the sound of her ball going into the cup)*
Yippee!

ANDERSON: Now my wife's beating me, Yukio.
What would the Seven Samurai say about that?

JULIA: They'd say you're not concentrating.

ANDERSON: The kid was just learning the ropes.

JULIA: You talk as if he's already gone.

ANDERSON: *(He putts and misses.)* Damn!

JULIA: Relax.

ANDERSON: One thing I've learned from this frigging
shore duty: You can't fight Washington.

JULIA: *You* can't, maybe.

ANDERSON: Don't tell me *you* can.

JULIA: I can certainly try.

ANDERSON: You're the one who wanted to send him
away.

JULIA: I know now that would just make him mad.

ANDERSON: *(He putts again and misses.)* Hell's bells!
(He putts again and we hear it go in.)

READER: Very good, Captain-san

ANDERSON: Yeah, yeah... So, what would you do?

JULIA: I'd telephone Emily, if you can get me a decent
long distance hookup. And I'd get her to call off the
dogs.

ANDERSON: It's a little late for that.

JULIA: Is it? I'll say we can handle this at the local level.

ANDERSON: Which means?

JULIA: Which means I'd do something about the girl.

ANDERSON: The girl.

JULIA: No one will get hurt, I promise.

ANDERSON: Except the girl.

JULIA: She'll land on her feet, Jim, I promise. Everyone will.

ANDERSON: I'd like to know how.

JULIA: *(Glancing at* STAGEHANDS*)* I'll spell it out as we play the back nine.

(Clack)

(Lights change.)

(Clack)

JULIA: So what do you think of my idea?

ANDERSON: *(Addressing the ball as if to drive)* What makes you so interested in him, Julia?

JULIA: I told you. I feel responsible.

ANDERSON: That's all?

JULIA: No, that's not all. I like him.

ANDERSON: Oh?

JULIA: He reminds me of home.

ANDERSON: Does he now?

JULIA: Oh, God, Jim! I'm old enough to be his—sister!

ANDERSON: I see.

JULIA: And concerned enough to care.

ANDERSON: Right. *(He swings.)* Shit. In a trap again.

JULIA: *(Setting up to drive)* I do wish, just once, you could tell me what's so wonderful about these Asian women.

ANDERSON: Wish I could.

JULIA: Or at least what's wrong with *us*? Is it because we read books, think thoughts, have opinions? Is that it? Is it because we do things in the world?

ANDERSON: Sometimes you do too much, Julia.

JULIA: When we think something's wrong, yes.

ANDERSON: Right, wrong. What makes you so goddam moral all the time?

JULIA: I suppose you'd prefer someone who sits back and bats her eyes while you bomb her country into golf courses?

ANDERSON: We marry you in the end. Isn't that enough?

JULIA: No it isn't, Jim. You know it isn't.... God, look at us! What a pair! You, a pacifist Navy pilot. And me... Who am I, Jim? *(She drives.)*

ANDERSON: You'd make a hell of a good Chief of Naval Operations.

(He goes off, followed by a STAGEHAND.)

JULIA: *(Looking out)* Damn! Much too much! *(To other STAGEHAND)* Now I'm in another bomb crater, Takeo!

READER: And Captain back in sands of Iwo Jima.

JULIA: What did you think of our little discussion, Takeo? As a Japanese man?

READER: I didn't hear, Mrs Captain-san.

JULIA: Sure you did. I'll bet you agree. American women must seem terribly aggressive.

READER: Ah no, Mrs Captain-san.

JULIA: Maybe we want to be like men. Or maybe it's more an American thing. Or maybe we're all that way, Takeo. Men, women, east, west. Were you that way, when you were winning the war?

READER: Captain waiting to play golf, Mrs Captain-san.

JULIA: Right. *(Starts off, stops)* At least tell me this, Takeo. Do Japanese men play golf with their wives?

READER: Never happen, Mrs Captain-san.

JULIA: Maybe that's the thing. They're smarter than we are—the wives, I mean. *(She goes off.)*

(Clack)

(Lights change.)

(SPARKY *comes on, angrily holding a piece of paper.*)

SPARKY: Is Captain Anderson here?

READER: He's in conference with the Admiral, sir.

SPARKY: Get him.

READER: Sir?

SPARKY: It's an emergency.

READER: Sir...

SPARKY: That's an order, sailor.

READER: Yes, sir.

SPARKY: I'll wait right here.

(Clack)

(ANDERSON *comes on in work khakis.*)

ANDERSON: What the hell?

SPARKY: I hear there's a staff slot available up in Tokyo.

ANDERSON: That's taken, Sparky.

SPARKY: Then find me another. Temporary duty.
Something.

ANDERSON: I am not the Princeton Placement Bureau,
friend.

SPARKY: Oh no? I hear different!

ANDERSON: Watch your attitude, Sparky!

SPARKY: *(Controlling himself)* Sir, I understand that
you're responsible, sir, for having my girl transferred
up to the Officer's Club in Tokyo, sir.

ANDERSON: You understand wrong.

SPARKY: *(Indicating piece of paper)* You signed the job
order.

ANDERSON: I sign lots of things. *(Starting back)* Now, if you'll excuse me...

SPARKY: For shit's sake, Jim! What is she? Some slave you can ship up the river?

ANDERSON: They gave her a promotion, Sparky.

SPARKY: Oh, sure. To the salad bar. At two thousand more a week.

ANDERSON: Two thousand yen is a lot of dough, Sparky.

SPARKY: Two thousand is less than ten bucks, Jim.

ANDERSON: Which is a lot to these people.

SPARKY: "These people, these people." She's my *girl*, Jim.

ANDERSON: They told me she agreed to go.

SPARKY: Or else be fired!

ANDERSON: The Steward says we're understaffed up there.

SPARKY: That's bullshit, Jim!

ANDERSON: I don't appreciate your tone of voice, Mr Watts.

SPARKY: O K. Pull rank on me now. Go ahead.

ANDERSON: Simmer down, now.

SPARKY: Want to court-martial me too?

ANDERSON: Just simmer down...

SPARKY: Yeah, well, I'm kind of pissed off!

ANDERSON: You can see her weekends.

SPARKY: That's not good enough.

ANDERSON: Commute, then. Use your goddam car.

SPARKY: This is your wife's doing, isn't it?

ANDERSON: At ease now.

SPARKY: Sure it is. She sits on the house committee.

ANDERSON: Steady now.

SPARKY: She's trying to break us up.

ANDERSON: My wife is not on the agenda here.

SPARKY: She's been farting around with my life ever since I got here.

ANDERSON: Did you hear what I just said, Lieutenant?

SPARKY: You owe me a transfer to Tokyo, sir.

ANDERSON: Owe you? *Owe* you? For Chrissake, who do you think I am? Some pimp, who makes it easier for you to fuck the local talent?

SPARKY: What a shitty thing to say, Jim!

ANDERSON: Get out of here, Lieutenant!

SPARKY: That was really shitty.

ANDERSON: Out!

SPARKY: I'm seeing the chaplain, sir.

ANDERSON: Try the psychiatrist first!

SPARKY: I'm telling the chaplain how you're coming between a man and his wife.

ANDERSON: Wife?

SPARKY: I'm marrying her, Jim.

ANDERSON: Sparky, my friend...

SPARKY: I've been to the Embassy, and picked up all the papers! We'll be tying the knot any day! *(He starts out, then turns back.)* Oh, hey! Say thanks to your wife! For bringing us together!

ANDERSON: *(Starting after him)* Lieutenant!... Mr Watts!... Sparky!

READER: The Admiral's waiting, sir!

ANDERSON: Tell the Admiral... *(Looks after SPARKY)* Tell him I'm.... *(Looks off)* Tell him I'm on my way. *(He goes off where he has come on.)*

(Clack and drum beats)

*(*STAGEHANDS *bring on bed.)*

*(*BOB *comes on in khakis and bare feet. He takes off his tie and belt, hands them to* STAGEHAND.*)*

(Other STAGEHAND *stands nearby, at attention, back to the audience, now wearing a Marine hat.)*

(Clack)

BOB: Well, whadya know? I actually get a Marine guard.

READER: Sir.

BOB: I'm O K, by the way. You don't need to keep such a close watch.

READER: Sir.

BOB: Take a break, if you want. Go hang out at the nurses' station. They've got the latest issue of Action Comics.

READER: Sir.

BOB: Look. No belt, no tie, no socks. I couldn't hang myself if I wanted to.

READER: Sir.

BOB: Oh, hell. Enough of this scintillating conversation. I'd like to read, please. O K if I read a book? See? Book? What do you suppose it is? *The Short Stories of Truman Capote?... The Life of Oscar Wilde?...* Nope. *(Reads title) Great Moments in Baseball.* See? Even after all this, I'm still a Red Sox fan. *(He sits on the bed and reads.)*

*(*SPARKY *comes on, in civilian clothes.)*

SPARKY: Hey, Bob.

BOB: *(Looking up)* Well, well.

SPARKY: *(Looking around)* The celebrity suite, huh?

BOB: It's not the Imperial Hotel.

SPARKY: I thought they might put you...

BOB: In the brig? Oh, God, no. I may have committed a heinous crime, but I'm still an officer in the U S Navy. I get the infirmary instead.

SPARKY: *(Indicating* READER*)* Dig the Marine guard.

BOB: That's because they think I might kill myself.

SPARKY: Do you want to?

BOB: Shit no. I'm hurt, I'm embarrassed, I'm angry. All that. But I'm not suicidal, O K?

SPARKY: O K. *(Pause)* So. What's the story, Bob?

BOB: You know the story, Sparky. Better than anyone.

SPARKY: I mean now. Where do you stand?

BOB: Stand? I don't stand. I fall. I'm guilty as sin, darkness, and death. They gave me a Bad Conduct Discharge.

SPARKY: They haven't announced it.

BOB: That's because your buddy the Captain wants the proceedings reviewed by the higher-ups.

SPARKY: Do you have a good defense counsel?

BOB: The best. This Ivy League Reservist. All bright-eyed and bushy-tailed. Reminds me of you, Sparks.

SPARKY: What does he say?

BOB: Say? He says Sayonara. Bye-bye.

SPARKY: What?

BOB: He got released early so he could make the start of Columbia Law School.

SPARKY: Jesus.

BOB: But before he left, he allowed as how they'd probably commute my sentence to a General Discharge.

SPARKY: A General Discharge?

BOB: To avoid any publicity about lax security and faggots in the Navy.

SPARKY: A General Discharge doesn't sound so bad, Bob.

BOB: No. It's not so bad. It will keep me from becoming President of General Motors.

SPARKY: Oh, well.

BOB: *(More seriously)* It will jeopardize my career at any executive level. But it could be worse, Sparky. *(Pause)* So. What brings you up to Tokyo?

SPARKY: She works here now.

BOB: Why?

SPARKY: They're trying to separate us.

BOB: Don't they like heterosexuals either?

SPARKY: They sure don't like mixed marriages.

BOB: You're married?

SPARKY: Trying to. They're throwing up all sorts of roadblocks.

BOB: What do your folks say?

SPARKY: Haven't you heard the screams from Lake Michigan?

BOB: I can imagine.

SPARKY: My old man even flew over. Took me to dinner at the Imperial Hotel. Read me the riot act.

BOB: Did he cut you off?

SPARKY: Threatened to. Totally. If I married her.

BOB: Wow.

SPARKY: He can be ruthless with my mother's money.

BOB: My dad died happy. With a picture of me in uniform right by his bed. Which is what he cared about. The uniform.

(Pause)

SPARKY: Are you sore at me, Bob? For putting the clamps on you that way.

BOB: You behaved like a responsible young naval officer. Quote unquote.

SPARKY: I hope you're having second thoughts about sleeping with guys, Bob. I hope you've learned that it can put you in a very vulnerable position.

BOB: (*Wryly*) I'll try to exercise better judgment, Sparky.

SPARKY: That might be a good idea.

BOB: The next time I'm approached by a person of the same sex, I'll make sure he's cleared for Top Secret.

(*They both laugh.*)

SPARKY: Anyway, we're friends?

BOB: Yes and no.

SPARKY: Why no?

BOB: Not in the same way, Sparks. I'm a different guy now.

SPARKY: You're the same to me, Bob.

BOB: Maybe. But not to myself. I'm on my own now. When I get back stateside, I haven't a clue about where to live or what to do with my life.

SPARKY: I know the feeling.

BOB: No, you don't, Sparks. This is very different.

SPARKY: O K. You're right.

BOB: I do know I'm tired of lying—making up fake girlfriends and shit.

SPARKY: Then don't do it, Bob.

BOB: Easy for you to say. You've got a real one.

SPARKY: If I've got the guts to follow through.

BOB: That'll be the tough part. Following through. For both you and me.

SPARKY: Right.

BOB: Well. Rots of ruck, buddy. *(He goes to "Marine Guard".)* Oh, Corporal.

READER: Sir.

BOB: I'd like to take my shower now.

(A STAGEHAND *hands him a towel.)*

READER: Sir.

BOB: I suppose you have to accompany me.

READER: Sir.

BOB: *(To* SPARKY*)* Isn't this weird? *(To Guard)* Do you provide the soap, or do I? *(He and the* STAGEHAND *go.)*

(Clack)

*(*SPARKY *remains. A* STAGEHAND *brings on an informal kimono, or* yukata, *and places it on the cot.)*

(Clack)

READER: *(Possibly using different voices)* Welcome back to the B O Q, Sparks.

SPARKY: Thanks.

READER: Sparky Watts here on a Saturday night? That's one for the books.

SPARKY: She's gone to Osaka to see her folks. Funny thing. They're even more against the marriage than mine are.

READER: Embassy still wrapping you in red tape?

SPARKY: I'm cutting through bit by bit.

READER: How's Bob? Still on a suicide watch?

SPARKY: Don't worry about Bob. He'll be O K.

(He begins to get undressed. A STAGEHAND *takes his clothes.)*

READER: How about hitting the beach with us, Sparks.

SPARKY: No, thanks.

READER: Boys' night out? Come on. This place is like a morgue.

SPARKY: Nope.

READER: Come on. A few brews at the Kit Kat? Frenchy is asking for you, buddy.

SPARKY: Tell her I'm bushed.

READER: *(Calls out, as if to the whole hall)* Anyone for the Kit Kat? *(No answer)* Guess the gang's all there. See ya in church, Sparks.

SPARKY: Amen. So long, guys.

(He sits on cot, turns on "radio". His gestures are echoed by the READER. Japanese music is heard. He turns the dial again. Static, then more Japanese music, then:)

READER: *(As radio)* W A F E, your Armed Forces Far East radio station, now brings you the number one hit from the U S A....

(We hear a current popular song. SPARKY lies on his cot, listening. JULIA comes on quietly. She carries a clutch purse.)

JULIA: *(As if at the door)* Anybody home?

SPARKY: *(Sitting up)* Mrs Anderson! *(Turns off "radio", quickly puts on his yukata)*

JULIA: My spies told me you were on base tonight. *(Coming in)* Jim and I were at this *endless* cocktail party at the Officers' Club when he was called up to Tokyo. So I had another gin and tonic. And thought—does this door lock?

SPARKY: You're off limits, Mrs Anderson.

JULIA: That's why I want to lock this goddam door.

SPARKY: Just turn the center doo-dab clockwise.

JULIA: Clockwise, which is the only way you turn... Did you get my note?

SPARKY: Yes.

JULIA: You didn't answer it.

SPARKY: I didn't want to.

JULIA: I called you at work. Several times. The yeoman kept saying you were away from your desk.

SPARKY: I wasn't.

JULIA: I know you weren't. That's why I had to track you to your lair.

SPARKY: If anyone sees you here, Mrs Anderson. There could be real trouble. For you and me both. No one can bring a girl in here.

JULIA: I'm not a girl.

SPARKY: Even the mama-sans who clean have to be out by five.

JULIA: I know the rules, Sparky. Or at least some of the rules. *(Pause)* I feel partly responsible for what's happened.

SPARKY: The Tokyo thing? Glad you admit it.

JULIA: I was simply trying to put the brakes on things.

SPARKY: It was none of your business, Mrs Anderson.

JULIA: I was acting on behalf of your family.

SPARKY: Much good it did you.

JULIA: I'm acting on behalf of them now.

SPARKY: Are you my psychiatrist, Mrs Anderson?

JULIA: I'm your friend, Sparky.

SPARKY: Some friend.

JULIA: And I'm also a friend, whether you know it or not, of your little Japanese companion.

SPARKY: Love that "little".

JULIA: Your girlfriend, then.

SPARKY: My fiancée.

JULIA: All right, all right.

SPARKY: Soon you can call her my wife.

JULIA: Whatever I call her, she is going to be absolutely destroyed in America.

SPARKY: Oh, no.

JULIA: Oh yes. She's quite lovely, Sparky. And very sweet. I understand all that. But I just can't see you squiring her around Milwaukee.

SPARKY: We won't live in Milwaukee.

JULIA: Or Cambridge, then, when you go to the Business School. Or at some East Side dinner party, when you start selling stocks in New York.

SPARKY: We're going to live in Hawaii.

JULIA: Hawaii?

SPARKY: That's where we plan to live.

JULIA: Jim said you hated Hawaii.

SPARKY: I didn't know any better. I've looked into it now. I've done research. Lots of guys with Japanese wives end up there. It's got all kinds of races living together, and nobody hassles you. It's the America of the future, Mrs Anderson.

JULIA: Aren't you being just a little bit silly, Sparky?

SPARKY: I don't think so.

JULIA: I know so. You're just doing this to spite your family.

SPARKY: That's your opinion.

JULIA: Yes it is, Sparky. I think you grew up in a very staid, very conservative environment—I know, because I've seen it. And lived it myself. And ran away from it, too—the cozy marriage, the house in the suburbs, the easy life—I know what fun it is to thumb your nose at all that.

SPARKY: You think that's all I'm doing? Having fun?

JULIA: I do. I think you're having a high old time kicking over the traces. That's what I think. And I also think you have no idea how lonely you can get when you cut yourself off from your roots.

SPARKY: You can think anything you want, Mrs Anderson.

JULIA: All right. Then I'll tell you something else. I think.... *(Pause)* Never mind.

SPARKY: Go on.

JULIA: All right, let's make this truth-telling time. I think you're also doing this to spite me.

SPARKY: Spite *you*?

JULIA: Yes, exactly. To spite me. Every time I've made an effort to bring you in, you've moved farther away.

SPARKY: Why would I want to do that, Mrs Anderson?

JULIA: Oh, that's easy, Sparky. I know the answer to that one.

SPARKY: Go on, then. Shoot.

JULIA: I think you're scared of me.

SPARKY: No offense, but I don't think so, Mrs Anderson.

JULIA: I think you are. I remind you of your Aunt Emily, and your mother, and all those girls at home you've been running away from.

SPARKY: That'll be the day.

JULIA: I'm sorry, but that's what I think. You've been running away from us, because we're strong and educated and not so easy to push around.

SPARKY: Lay off, Mrs Anderson.

JULIA: And on another level, a deeper level, you know you can never really get away from us, no matter how far you roam.

SPARKY: Oh, yes?

JULIA: Oh, yes. Because you know we can give you more, in the long run.

SPARKY: Oh is that it?

JULIA: Yes, that's it, Sparky. You're avoiding the issue now, but money says you'll see the light, in the end.

SPARKY: Never happen. *Neba hachi, tomodachi!*

JULIA: We'll see, we'll see.

SPARKY: You're pretty sure of stuff, aren't you, Mrs Anderson?

JULIA: No, I'm not. Not at all, these days. But in this case, I can speak with some confidence, because....

(Pause)

SPARKY: Because what.

JULIA: Because I'm avoiding things, too.

SPARKY: Oh, yes?

JULIA: Oh, yes. I'm avoiding the fact that I'm attracted to you.

SPARKY: Hey, Mrs Anderson...

JULIA: No, I am. I admit it. I'm attracted to you. Maybe it's because you remind me of all those sweet boys I used to kiss goodnight under the lights outside our dorm at Smith, before they drove back to New Haven or Williamstown. Or maybe you make me remember those other boys, in their fresh new uniforms, whom I met after work at P J Clarke's in New York, and whom I also kissed, kissed goodnight, before they went off to war.

SPARKY: Mrs Anderson...

JULIA: I said *maybe*, Sparky. Because I don't know all the answers. I do know how it feels to keep everything bottled up inside till you think you're going to explode, and so you try frantically to throw your attention onto something else, your job maybe, or when that goes sour, another person. But it doesn't work, and soon you're making someone miserable, and yourself even more so. So you get up at night, and wander from room to room, thinking of the one you could really love, wondering where is he now, is he with his girl, and why is he with her when he could be with me, and all you want to do is see him occasionally, just occasionally see him, and touch him, and dance with him, maybe just dance with him, that was fun, wasn't it, the dancing, and.... *(Pause)* Oh, dear... *(Pause)* Oh, God. Now I've done it now, haven't I? Now I've really spilled the beans.

SPARKY: *(Going toward her)* Mrs Anderson...

JULIA: Don't come near me, please.

SPARKY: I know what you're saying, Mrs Anderson.

JULIA: You couldn't possibly.

SPARKY: No, I do. I'm with you on this one. I think you're a very attractive woman, Mrs Anderson, and I think about you a lot.

JULIA: Then call me Julia, you shit.

SPARKY: O K, Julia. Fair enough. Julia.

(He touches her, holds her, then kisses her. She breaks it off.)

JULIA: Thank you, Sparky.

SPARKY: *(Indicating the cot)* Would you like me to...

JULIA: No, thank you. *(She gets up.)*

SPARKY: No, seriously. We could....

JULIA: I said thank you, no. As someone once told me, I have no follow-through. *(Pause)* Now. Please. Check and see if the coast is clear, please.

(He goes to check the "hall." She speaks more to herself.)

JULIA: I suddenly have this vision of you squiring *me* around Milwaukee. Or living with *me* in Cambridge, or taking *me* to one of those East Side dinner parties when you move to New York. And it all seems equally dumb.

SPARKY: *(Indicating the hall)* It's O K out there.

JULIA: Then anchors away. *(Starts out)* Do you love this girl?

SPARKY: Oh, yes. I think I do. I hope I do.

JULIA: Then I hope you'll be very happy. I mean that.

(She kisses him on the cheek and goes. He stands in his kimono, watching her go.)

(Clack)

(He goes off.)

(Lights change.)

(ANDERSON enters.)

READER: A new batch of orders from Washington, sir. Primarily for reservists. Early release from active duty.

(STAGEHANDS give him orders, then remove the bed.)

ANDERSON: *(Thumbing through the orders)* Anyone we know? *(He finds SPARKY's orders.)* Folsom.

READER: Sir.

ANDERSON: Send a cable to the Bureau of Personnel, Washington, D C.

READER: Aye, aye, sir.

ANDERSON: *(Dictating)* Request cancellation BUPERS discharge order 6530 dash Dog. Reasons follow: One: Lieutenant (j.g.) Watts has begun to display considerable competence in the area of logistic plans.

His recent report on Da Nang harbor in South Vietnam is a model of precise description and may prove useful should the situation there deteriorate. Two: Watts has indicated an interest in attending flight school and a future career in military service. Therefore, it would be of benefit both to the Navy and to Lieutenant Watts if he were encouraged to serve out his.... *(Pause)* If he were encouraged... *(Pause)* If he made the commitment himself, Folsom.

READER: Sir?

ANDERSON: *(Handing the orders to a* STAGEHAND*)* Distribute these orders to the various subdepartments.

READER: Aye aye, sir.

(ANDERSON exits.)

(Clack)

(SPARKY comes on, isolated in light. He is finishing dressing in his winter blues.)

SPARKY: These are my Blues. They're called Dress Blues. We wear them in winter.

READER: You go now, Sparky-san?

SPARKY: Yes, but just for a little while. Remember? I told you.... O K, now. The car. It's yours now. See? There's the registration. See where I wrote your name? I've parked it in the garage near Kamakura. It's all paid up till I get back. O K?... And that's my sister's address in Milwaukee. When you write me letters, send them to her. That way my mother and father won't have to know. O K? ... And that's your passbook for the Nippon Bank. Look inside. See? Plenty of money for the rent. And a sukoshi more, in case...in case you need it. O K?... O K?...

(Clack)

(ANDERSON enters as large panoramic map of the Pacific and Southeast Asia drops into place.)

SPARKY: Are you busy, sir?

ANDERSON: *(Signing a document)* Pretending to be. *(Indicating his uniform)* I see you're all set to go.

SPARKY: Not really, sir. There's still personal stuff.

ANDERSON: Your orders are cut, friend. The Navy is beginning to weed out the reservists.

SPARKY: Why?

ANDERSON: The truce in Korea seems to be holding. The partition of Vietnam is somewhat successful. Russia has backed off on Berlin. The world looks reasonably safe, Sparky Watts, so the Navy feels it can let you go. With luck, you'll only miss the first few weeks of Business School.

SPARKY: I'm not going to Business School, sir.

ANDERSON: Then some other institute of higher earning.

SPARKY: I want to sign up for another tour of duty, Jim.

ANDERSON: You can do that back in the States.

SPARKY: Why not right here, right now?

ANDERSON: Because the Navy has discovered that overseas reenlistments are mostly made for the wrong reasons.

SPARKY: Then how about a week's delay? I need time to think about my life, Jim.

ANDERSON: You'll get time, Sparky. You'll get a long, boring, propeller flight in an old D C-6 across the vast reaches of the Pacific Ocean. You can think your ass off. And you can keep thinking during two weeks' basket leave in San Francisco while you wait for your car.

SPARKY: The car stays, Jim.

ANDERSON: It's against regulations to sell it.

SPARKY: I put it in her name.

ANDERSON: Can she drive?

SPARKY: I'll teach her, when I come back.

ANDERSON: If you come back.

SPARKY: Oh, I'll be back, sir. That's for sure. I fit in here.

ANDERSON: I think you're scared, Sparky.

SPARKY: Scared?

ANDERSON: Scared you'll fit in there.

SPARKY: Why, that's...ridiculous.

ANDERSON: Then there's no problem. I've designated you official escort for your misbegotten pal.

(BOB *comes on, carrying a bag. He sits and reads a book, as if in an airport waiting room.*)

SPARKY: Don't worry about Bob.

ANDERSON: I'll stop worrying about Bob when he's out of the Navy. What flight did we put you on?

SPARKY: MATS Flight 580, out of Atsugi.

ANDERSON: My wife's on the same plane.

(JULIA *comes on in a traveling suit. She sits waiting near Bob, possibly doing a crossword puzzle*)

SPARKY: Your wife? A vacation, sir?

ANDERSON: That's it. A vacation... From me... American women are complicated, Sparky. This is the second one I've lost.

SPARKY: I'm sorry, sir.

ANDERSON: She wants to return to civilian life.

SPARKY: Why?

ANDERSON: She says the Navy makes her say and do things she's sorry for later. She cited her behavior toward you.

SPARKY: Me, sir?

ANDERSON: She feels she intruded in your affairs.

SPARKY: She wanted to remind me of what I was missing.

ANDERSON: Did she succeed?

SPARKY: She did.

ANDERSON: Anything I should know that I don't?

SPARKY: No, sir.

ANDERSON: That's what she said. No. *(Pause)* She thinks I don't love her, Sparky. *(Pause)* She thinks I love someone else. *(Pause)* She's right.

SPARKY: That girl in Manila?

ANDERSON: The Navy. I love the Navy.

SPARKY: True enough.

ANDERSON: So. She's flying the coop. And so am I.

(A STAGEHAND *brings on his flight jacket. It is bulky, worn, and decorated with colorful insignia. He puts it on.)*

ANDERSON: My new orders came in. Operations officer on the *Forrestal*. Seventh Fleet.

SPARKY: Congratulations, sir.

ANDERSON: We'll be patrolling the Straits of Formosa. Protecting two little Taiwanese islands called Quemoy and Matsu from a dastardly attack by the Chinese, who owned them in the first place.

SPARKY: Will you be flying, sir?

ANDERSON: Not much. Too old. But I'll be launching planes and bringing them in. And working with a canted deck and steam catapults for the first time. And nuclear power! It's the real Navy, Sparky. Not all this messy shit ashore. *(Checks watch)* I'll have to kick you out, friend. I've got things to do.

SPARKY: I'll look you up when I get back.

ANDERSON: And when will that be, Sparky Watts?

SPARKY: Almost immediately.

ANDERSON: Almost is a big word.

SPARKY: I want to go to Milwaukee.

ANDERSON: Oh?

SPARKY: To touch base with the folks.

ANDERSON: Ah.

SPARKY: Then maybe a quick trip to New York.

ANDERSON: New York?

SPARKY: Just to catch up with my gang. And see the Dodgers win the Series.

ANDERSON: Oh, right.

SPARKY: But then I'm signing up for another stint in the Far East. One way or another, I'll get back, Jim. You'll be my best man and hand me the ring.

ANDERSON: I'll be long since gone.

SPARKY: I'll find you, Jim. We'll rendezvous in that bar in Saigon.

ANDERSON: I hope not there, pal. But I'll miss you just the same. Now shove off.

SPARKY: (As they shake hands) Hey, Jim, give me one more day here! Twenty-four hours! Special permission. Please!

ANDERSON: I said shove off, Lieutenant.

SPARKY: (Putting on his hat, saluting) Aye, aye, sir.

(SPARKY goes upstage, gets an overnight bag, waits as if at the door of a plane. ANDERSON walks upstage. We hear the sound of plane engines starting up. JULIA and BOB rise and walk as if about to board. The STAGEHANDS adjust the stools to become seats in a plane. BOB and JULIA walk past SPARKY. BOB gives SPARKY an ambiguous nod and takes his seat. JULIA forces a polite smile and takes her seat. SPARKY enters the "plane", settles into his own seat, stage center.)

READER: Stand by for takeoff.

(The three passengers fasten their "seat-belts". The sound of engines gets louder. The three lean back simultaneously during "take-off". Then they look out the "window" as the sound of Jo Stafford singing drowns out the engine noise:)

"Fly the ocean in a silver plane,
See the jungle when it's wet with rain...

(The backdrop or screen of a Japanese scene is replaced by the original seascape. Then the American flag is projected onto this drop, or onto the floor.)

"But remember, darling till you're home again,
You Belong to Me."

(The lights dim on BOB *reading,* JULIA *looking out and down.* ANDERSON *remains upstage. The music returns to the Japanese flute sound from the beginning of the play. Lights isolates* SPARKY *and the* READER *as he watches her carefully close her script. Then she gives a final clack.)*

(Blackout)

END OF PLAY

BROADWAY PLAY PUBLISHING INC

TOP TEN BEST SELLING FULL-LENGTH PLAYS AND FULL-LENGTH PLAY COLLECTIONS

AVEN'U BOYS

THE BROTHERS KARAMAZOV

THE IMMIGRANT

ONE FLEA SPARE

ON THE VERGE

PLAYS BY TONY KUSHNER
(CONTAINING A BRIGHT ROOM CALLED DAY,
THE ILLUSION, & SLAVS!)

PLAYS BY AISHAH RAHMAN
(CONTAINING THE MOJO AND THE SAYSO,
UNFINISHED WOMEN...,
& ONLY IN AMERICA)

PRELUDE TO A KISS

TALES OF THE LOST FORMICANS

TO GILLIAN ON HER 37TH BIRTHDAY

"...this poignant new play is a welcome reminder of A R Gurney's gliding dialogue and structural elegance, as well as the troubled, rueful heart that informs all his work."
Ben Brantley, *The New York Times*

"A play that does everything right.
The new drama by A R Gurney looks at who Americans were in the mid-1950s—a few Americans, anyway—and how they behaved out in those vast stretches of the world over which they had sway, and what their songs and movies and slang expressions and values were.
The story centers on four U S Navy people (one a Navy wife) stationed at a base in Japan in 1954 and 1955....
This subtle, tender play is, I think, Gurney's best work. It's John Cheever-meets-James Michener and it's a critical elegy for a long-vanished American view of life."
Donald Lyons, *New York Post*

"It is no coincidence that the movie playing at the overseas Officer's Club in A R Gurney's new play FAR EAST is *From Here to Eternity*: the 1953 Pearl Harbor drama starring Burt Lancaster as a rugged Army sergeant who has a torrid affair with the restless wife of his commander....
This deliciously wry play...."
Amy Gamerman, *The Wall Street Journal*

"East meets 'WASP' in this love story, which has been given a highly theatrical, quasi-Kabuki-style production. The result is an intriguing scrapbook of mid-1950's attitudes, opinions, prejudices, and social conventions."
Michael Kuchwara, *Associated Press*

Cover art compliments of Lincoln Center   I S B N 0-88145-161-4

Echinacea
The Immune Herb!

BY CHRISTOPHER HOBBS, L. Ac.